This is How it
Feels to be City

Supporting Manchester City

Will Linsdell

This is How it Feels to be City

Supporting Manchester City

Will Linsdell

DB PUBLISHING

First published in Great Britain in 2012 by The Derby Books Publishing Company Limited, 3 The Parker Centre, Derby, DE21 4SZ.

Revised first edition 2013 by DB Publishing, an imprint of JMD Media.

ISBN 9781780913292

Printed and bound by Copytech (UK) Limited, Peterborough.

Contents

Acknowledgements

There are a few people that I would like to thank in helping me on my journey to writing this book.

My Dad, Terry, who instilled the football bug into me and drove me to my first City match. My two brothers, Kev & Ed, who in following rival teams (Leeds & Ipswich) brought an early sense of competition into our Devon household. My sister Jackie who provided the nephews to enable me to pass on my passion and to those nephews (Martyn & Josh) who readily bought into the concept of City.

To John Burfield, the only other City fan that attended my senior school in Devon and who remains a City buddy over 30 years later.

To Stuart Hamilton & Jon Kenny who formed the South West Supporters Club with me so that for a few seasons in the '80s & '90s I got to see City 30-40 times a season from my home in mid Devon. To fellow Blues Harvey Clarke, Mad Lawrence, Geoff Coope, Pete Riley, Michael Owen and Bill & Nick Hewitt who joined me on those trips and made them so special, win or lose.

Most of all I would like to thank my wife Rania who has to put up with my unreasonable behaviour in loving City. My need to catch a game whatever the occasion or whatever country we are in. My days of thinking about nothing else but the match leading up to a big game. My sulky mood when we lose. She puts up with it all and is now even the proud owner of a new City shirt with Mancini on the back!

Lastly, thank you City. You have and always will be OUR club, for richer, for poorer, in bad times as well as good.

Introduction

Forty-four years since their last top League title, Manchester City were crowned champions of England in 2012 for only the third time in their long history, pipping local rivals Manchester United on goal difference in the process.

In 1999 they won a far less coveted trophy awarded for winning the Division Two promotion Play-off Final and thus propelling the club back up to the 'heights' 'of English football's second tier.

At about the same time, the aforementioned local rivals were completing an unprecedented victorious treble of the English title and Cup as well as being crowned champions of Europe.

Without City's 1999 victory, it is highly likely that 2012 triumph would never have happened.

Modern City may be light years away from the humble outfit of just over a decade ago, but there are plenty of parallels to be drawn alongside all of the contrasts.

This book captures the dramas and the emotion produced by the two winning squads, culminating in unbelievable final acts, as witnessed through the eyes of two lifelong City fans, 40-something Will and nephew Martyn, 17 years his junior. Feel their hopes, fears, nerves, disappointment, resignation, exultation and final relief.

The Author

Will

Will is frequently asked why he supports City, raised in Devon, no connections to Manchester, no parental pressure or inducement, certainly not a glory hunter. So why?

Will likes to think that City choose you. He must have worn some sort of Harry Potteresque sporting headgear at an age when he couldn't think rationally past, 'I'm hungry or it hurts' and somebody somewhere must have bellowed, 'it's Manchester City for you!'

Perhaps it was the light blue and white bobble hat his mum stuck on his blond bonce when he was a toddler. Who knows?

Will is certainly pleased that the second word was City, what if there had been devilment in that hat and he had been condemned to the House of the Serpents? OMG, unimaginable!

If the truth be told, although it was 1972 that the union had been sealed, it was not until 1975 that a real liking for football developed. Inspired by his Dad's beloved Hammers blowing victory bubbles at Wembley, one of the very few games to be shown live on TV in those days, Will subconsciously decided to take a proper interest.

If football could make his Dad that happy, surely it could only be a good thing? A few days later, the TV showed another live game, this time the Home International between England and Scotland at Wembley once more. A rampant home side thrashed the Scots 5-1, including a wonderful strike by Colin Bell of…Manchester City. The marriage was consummated. That was it, 'City till I die!'

Will went for it in as big a style as a Devon boy could in those days. Subscription to *Shoot!* magazine, *MOTD*, *The Big Match* and *Harry Carpenter's Sportsnight*. The real excitement was 4.40pm on a Saturday afternoon with *Grandstand's* teleprinter or final score on *World of Sport*. He used to fret – won't that wrestling ever finish to release Dickie Davis onto our screens to let us in on those latest scores and results?

Sports Report on Radio Two. Bliss!

A yearly scrapbook bound in *Shoot's* City team group was kept – newspaper reports on every game, results meticulously recorded, players rated based on reports and TV highlights (Bell always got at least 9!), player profiles, etc.

He longed for City to get to the FA Cup Final. In those days it was the only domestic game that was shown live, simultaneously on BBC1 and ITV. It was always the Beeb in their house and the TV schedule started at 8am showing the players having their breakfast, followed by a stroll around their hotel grounds and at about midday trailing the team as they clambered aboard the team bus for the journey to Wembley.

You also had the delight of popular programmes of the day adapted to fit the two finalists. Shows such as; *FA Cup Mastermind* and *FA Cup It's a Knockout*.

Sadly by the time City got to the Final in 1981, the schedule had been shortened and the chance of sitting in the black chair to answer Magnus's questions on City had disappeared.

All those years that Will had watched Southampton, Ipswich, West Ham, Liverpool and worst of all United fans having all that fun, only for it to be pulled when City made it. Gutted!

In 1976 City did win the League Cup, which was to be their last major piece of silverware for 36 years. It had cost them the prime years of Colin Bell (terrible injury in the fourth round thrashing of United) and as the junior cup competition it only received 40 minutes of recorded highlights on the Sunday, but it was still a cup.

In 1977 the popular BBC weekday news programme *Nationwide* fronted by subsequently outed party animal Frank Bough (of *Grandstand* fame), adopted City as their team. The club granted them unprecedented behind the scenes access for four or five years. The agreement was that the cameras were allowed everywhere except for the players' bath.

What a treat for a young City fan living down south – pictures beamed into the living room of players training, board meetings, transfer discussions, match day preparations, etc. The programme heavily featured Colin Bell's long and ultimately doomed fight to regain his supreme fitness. Pivotal events such as the prodigal return of Malcolm Allison in 1978, his sacking in 1980 and appointment of John Bond as replacement were played out to millions and one wide-eyed Devonian.

This was the first time that Will believed that City were a special club. Nothing since has changed his mind.

City were then and always will be a family club. Tony Book, City's manager in the mid to late '70s was Will's pseudo uncle and chairman Peter Swales his beleaguered imaginary grandfather.

Will first saw City in the flesh in February 1978 at Bristol City. To see his heroes close up for the first time was a momentous occasion. At that time, City were stocked full of internationals, top of the League and on a 17-game unbeaten run.

Bristol City were a team of good honest pros without stars and were engaged in a relegation battle. Bristol won 1-0.

His first lesson in following Manchester City – expect the unexpected, don't get your hopes too high.

City finished second the previous season. They would have won the League if they had not conceded a last minute own goal against eventual champions Liverpool. The phrase typical City was coined.

In 1982 Will's nephew Martyn was born. A year later City were relegated from the top flight after 17 consecutive seasons plying their trade there.

Martyn had already been inducted unknowingly into the City supporter academy – an uncle's unilateral decision of kindness or cruelty?

City then became somewhat a yoyo club with four promotions and relegations between the top two Leagues until in 1998 the unthinkable happened and City were relegated to the third tier for the first time in their history...

Martyn - The indoctrinated nephew/author's sidekick

It was a player with no connection whatsoever to Manchester City that caused Martyn to (finally) fall in love with football.

His first City game came as a six-year-old in 1989, but if he's honest the only thing he really remembers from that day were the inflatables, the pre-Taylor report terraces and the motorway service station sausage and chips on the way home.

Will took him to several more games over the next few years but, although he enjoyed the road trips and days out with his uncle, the actual football itself passed him by.

Martyn faintly remembers his first experience of Maine Road, the postage stamp sized club shop and what (little) he could see from his Main (Family) Stand (no swearing Uncle Will!) seat. He recalls kicking an errant cardboard box in a token show of frustrated solidarity on their way out of Highbury after being thumped 4-0.

Most of all, he remembers waiting outside the team hotel when City came to Exeter to play in a testimonial game* and leaving highly impressed by just how tall Niall Quinn was, and the fact that City winger David White addressed his (apparently semi-famous in South West City supporting circles) uncle by his first name as he breezed past.

However, this really is the entirety of his memories of Manchester City before he turned 12. He remembers no goals, no passages of play, no celebrations and no tears. Football and City were just concepts that he knew he 'liked', even if he couldn't tell you why. Will told him he was a City fan, so he was one.

Ray Houghton changed his life. His winning goal for the Republic of Ireland against Italy in New Jersey during the 1994 World Cup woke something in him that until that moment had lain dormant.

Martyn and family had moved from their home in Devon to live on an army barracks on the Hampshire and West Sussex border with his Mum's new husband. The kids who lived on the army base were ALL football fans, and it was very clear to him early on that he was going to have to stop watching so much WWF wrestling and go out and play football if he was going to make new friends.

Obviously a big part of that was showing your allegiances, and Martyn was only too happy to tell the other boys he was a City fan, even though this meant he was something of a fraud.

He hadn't got the shirt, didn't collect the stickers and didn't even have an idea how they were doing in the League. Not so great as it turns out, but this didn't bother Martyn, as he still wasn't emotionally 'involved'.

Seeing Jack Charlton's motley mishmash of honest pros defeat the glittering stars from Serie A changed all that.

Even as (relatively) long ago as 1994 you could not see top division football on terrestrial television. The World Cup that summer was his first real window into how much potential for drama and poetry there was in this sport.

The fact that England weren't present probably made it even better, as he was able to watch the tournament unfold without partisan blinkers on, and just enjoy it.

After Roberto Baggio's penalty had sailed over the bar in Pasadena, gifting Brazil an unprecedented fourth World Cup win, Martyn was completely sold on the sport.

Now he had to make up for lost time!

*Footnote – this was Steve Neville's testimonial game on a Monday night and after a reception at the Royal Clarence Hotel, Will ended up in an Exeter night club with City's players and manager Peter Reid. The club had opened its doors especially for the night.

The players stayed drinking until 2am (there was still a final League game to play on the Saturday!) before it was closing time and time to leave.

Will witnessed City players Tony Coton, Adrian Heath, Wayne Clarke and Alan Harper being led into a local pub that was being unlocked to allow the players to continue to unwind.

Feeling inebriated himself, Will called out, 'don't go in there, it's a real dive'. Coton turned round and bellowed, 'don't worry, I've been chucked out of far worse places than this before'.

Having witnessed him drinking pints with whisky chasers all night and knowing some of the stories of his wild days earlier in his career at Birmingham, Will didn't doubt it for one minute!

1

THE BUILD UP

Route 98,
The Downhill Road

To understand how City made it into the third tier, you have to go back to the Nationwide days of the late '70s.

At that time, City were one of England's Big Five with Liverpool, Arsenal, Manchester United and Everton. England internationals such as Peter Barnes, Joe Corrigan, Dave Watson, Mike Channon and Gary Owen were all in the City squad. Scotland regulars Willie Donachie and Asa Hartford augmented this array of Anglo talent.

These were the days before the English Leagues opened their doors to the world's stars of today. Every team was made up almost entirely of players from the British Isles and the strongest teams had most of the best ones. City under Tony Book's management had finished second then fourth in the two seasons prior to the 1978-79 season. In 1978-79 City reached the quarter-finals of the UEFA Cup (Europe's second most prestigious trophy), knocking out the likes of Standard Liege and AC Milan along the way, but underperformed in the League finishing a way below par 15th.

City chairman Swales decided action was needed to bring City the title he craved. He believed that the man to deliver it was Malcolm Allison. Big Mal as he was known had masterminded City's last League title triumph in 1968, when he was the brash young coach with visionary ideas. The Eric Morecambe character complimenting manager Joe Mercer's Ernie Wise approach.

Book was moved upstairs and Big Mal arrived in a blaze of cigar smoking and champagne swilling publicity to take charge.

Fourteen-year-old Will thought this a great move. The newspapers were dominated by City stories, manna from heaven for an exiled Blue. The honeymoon lasted about five minutes as Will's favourite stars were flogged off one by one.

He watched from afar in disbelief as home grown stars Peter Barnes and Gary Owen were despatched to West Brom, captain and England centre-back Dave Watson was sold to Werder Bremen in Germany and Asa Hartford, Scotland's midfield dynamo joined champions Nottingham Forest.

But at least we replaced those seasoned internationals with equally decorated players, right? No!

Michael Robinson, an unknown striker from lowly Preston was brought in for an incredible £750,000, a new captain was brought in, in the shape of Yugoslav Dragoslav Stepanovic who of course did not speak a word of English! Steve MacKenzie arrived from Crystal Palace for a whopping £250,000, a huge fee at the time for a 17-year-old who had yet to play a first team game.

Kevin Reeves, an England B international striker was recruited for an eye-watering £1 million. However, the deal that was to sum up Allison's second coming was the near £1.5 million signing of Steve Daley from Wolves. We had smashed the British transfer record for a player that was not even a full international and was to be sold a year or so later for a loss of £1.2 million! Typical City.

Will was heartbroken. His bedroom wall once adorned with posters of all his heroes was now virtually bare – it took *Shoot!* months to catch up with Allison's wheeling and dealing.

That season City finished 17th – despite shelling out millions, they had had a worse season than the previous one.

The real damage, however, was to the bank balance. In chasing the dream, Swales had mortgaged City to the hilt. The club was SKINT and despite that Centenary Cup Final appearance in 1981, the cracks were there for all to see.

Somehow City scraped together another million or so to buy Trevor Francis, but his stay lasted just one season. He was by all accounts a superstar of the time and had in fact been the country's first £1 million player when he left Birmingham for Forest, famously scoring the winner in the European Cup Final for Brian Clough's team.

Will had one chance to see Francis in the flesh. The game was March 1982 and was in fact Will's first ever game at Maine Road, just two weeks after he had started his first ever job. No doubting where his priorities lay once he had earned his first wage packet!

The train journey from Devon to Manchester was awkward to say the least, involving three changes and taking seven hours, not helped by a 'jumper' between Plymouth and Exeter, but it would be worth it to see Clever Trevor in a blue shirt, one of our few current England internationals of that era.

Unbelievably Francis was sent off after 41 minutes for feigning a head-butt towards an Everton defender. Just typical! The journey home seemed to take an eternity after that but at least City got a point on Will's first ever Manchester trip.

Prior to the 1982-83 season, there was a fire sale of the best players including Francis and City spiralled to relegation in 1983. That was despite winning their first three games and briefly leading the table. John Bond resigned well before demotion was confirmed.

The sight or sound of David Pleat still brings back that painful memory of him prancing across the Maine Road pitch in delight as his Luton team secured safety at City's expense with a late single goal victory. He looked like a demented morris dancer without the bells!

A team of youngsters, free transfers and a couple of £30,000 signings some-how clawed their way back to the big time two seasons later but relegation soon followed again.

Swales was known as the assassin in the '80s as managers came and went on an almost seasonal basis, all failing to come up to Swales' lofty expectations, still lofty despite City having no money to invest in decent players.

There was no choice but to rely on homegrown talent and in 1986 City unearthed their salvation. The team that won the FA Youth Cup contained over half a dozen youngsters that would go on to star in the top flight. Players such as Andy Hinchcliffe, David White, Steve Redmond, Paul Lake, Paul Moulden and Ian Brightwell.

They were all thrust into the City first team under Mel Machin, where they thrived alongside experienced pros like John Gidman and Neil McNab.

In 1987 this team thrashed Huddersfield 10-1 with White, Paul Stewart and Tony Adcock all grabbing hat-tricks. Swales vowed that none of the youngsters would ever be sold.

Most of them were of course, while Paul Lake, the cream of the crop, had his promising career cruelly crushed early through injury; his autobiography entitled *I'm Not Really Here*, is both harrowing and superb. The truth was that if he hadn't been injured he would have been flogged to Liverpool anyway.

The promised salvation never materialised and young Will and even younger Martyn had their hopes dashed once more. They both identified with the City team as the '80s turned into the '90s. Manchester was the centre of British and even World youth culture at the time and City's young, vibrant team fitted the bill perfectly.

This was the time of the Manchester music scene, when Oasis v Blur was bigger than City v United; the time of the Roses, the Mondays and the Inspirals.

Oasis, fronted by the City mad Gallagher brothers (more on them later) went from strength to strength, while City went from relative strength to near oblivion.

Despite the odd high – promotion back to Division One, beating United 5-1, an FA Cup quarter-final, finally getting rid of perennial bad penny Swales; the odd big name star (Keith Curle, Niall Quinn, Gergiou Kinkladze, Uwe Rosler), there were plenty of lows – regular United thrashings, relegation, going backwards with Franny (former City playing hero Francis Lee had replaced Swales to fanfares and high expectations), the sale of favourites Quinn, Rosler and Kinkladze and plenty of decidedly poor players like Michael Frontzek, Kare Ingebrigtsen, Kit Symons, Ged Brannan, Jim Whitley, Alfons Groenendijk, Rae Ingram (we could go on and on).

In 1989 Will got together with several other West Country City fans to form the South West Manchester City Supporters' Club. With a catchment area from Falmouth to South Wales, they ran minibus trips to every match and Will went to most of them. There were not too many season tickets holders in Devon but Will was one.

This was the time of fanzines (the brilliant King of the Kippax had been paramount in uniting the Devon Blue exiles) and the City generated craze of taking inflatables to matches.

Will used to take along a giant inflatable rhinoceros called Rhino Gayle in deference to then City captain Brian Gayle (it used to scare the family cat senseless when fully inflated!)

This was an unequalled period of terrace humour with City fans the self-deprecating kings of comedy, complete with a giant Frankenstein resplendent in XXL City shirt, countless bananas and the odd paddling pool. The football may have been dire in the most part but you were always guaranteed entertainment following City.

At the end of the 1995-96 season, City under Alan Ball were relegated once more to the second tier of football. Francis Lee had headhunted 1966 World Cup winner Ball, much to the author's chagrin. Alongside most supporters, we associated Ball with managerial failure.

He may have been a fine player but as a manager he had suffered relegations with Portsmouth, Stoke and Exeter City (our local team). He completed an unwanted quadruple with City.

Ball was entrusted with bouncing City back up to the Big Time. For the entire pre-season schedule of matches, he played 6ft 4in Niall Quinn up front, only to sell him just before the season kicked off and replace him with 5ft 5in Paul Dickov!

Three games into the season City travelled to Stoke – Will had never witnessed anything like it. Ball was loathed by Stoke for recently relegating them to the third tier as their own manager and the atmosphere was really hostile towards him.

Manchester City struggled to defeat and you had the unprecedented situation of both sets of fans constantly catcalling the unfortunate Ball. 'Alan Ball's a football genius', rang out from every stand. Lee promptly removed Ball from his post, probably more in kindness than panic.

City became a laughing stock, sorely testing the faith of the authors and most City supporters.

City coach and ex-playing star Asa Hartford was installed as caretaker manager before ex-United star Steve Coppell was brought in as manager. He lasted barely a month before quitting; his self-appointed assistant (and Graham Taylor's England yes man) Phil Neal became caretaker before City finally settled on Forest manager Frank Clark as their new team leader.

Paul Dickov had had eight different managers in three months, being managed by Rioch, Rice and Wenger at Arsenal before the City debacle! He surely checked his deodorant on more than one occasion!

This was an embarrassing time to be a City fan. We were the butt of national jokes with Chris Evans on Radio One's influential breakfast show having an almost daily City pun.

Being City fans though, we didn't stay embarrassed for long and were soon making the jokes at our own expense.

Will even got a £1 ginger loan from Evans. Listeners were encouraged to write in and request a £1 loan, with the funniest and craziest read out on air.

Will requested a quid to buy a book of Manchester City Christmas raffle tickets that he was having difficulty selling. The first prize was a day at Chester races as guest of Francis Lee and second prize was something like a sky blue City kettle!

He had explained that he had given £4 worth away as Christmas presents, but had been unable to shift the last pound's worth.

Evans readily read out the letter and sent Will his pound. This led to daily countdowns as the big draw approached, relentless mickey-taking out of the 'many fabulous prizes' and Evans and his breakfast show team debating what they would do with the prizes if they won.

If the City PR Department had any nous they would have fixed it for Evans and the team to win first prize and shown the club as able to mirror their own fans in enjoying a joke at our own expense.

Instead Evans lamented his £1 loss and got listeners that won prizes to call in and explain whether the City alarm clock that they had won was now taking pride of place on their bedside table! Nobody ever did admit to spending a day at the races with Franny.

Promotion favourites City limped to 14th place that season, but worse was to follow.

City were again favourites to go up – surely the previous season had been a blip?

Unfortunately not. City were consistently flirting with relegation all season. Frank Clark's tenure ended in February 1998 with City languishing in the lower reaches of the League.

Former City number nine Joe Royle was entrusted with the dozen or so games left to save City from relegation. He narrowly failed. In a twist of extreme irony, Ball had returned to Portsmouth in January 1998 and inspired them to survive above City by a single point, with his other August 1996 tormentors Stoke also relegated.

Tears flowed in the Linsdell household. We thrashed Stoke 5-2 on the final day but it was out of our hands. Portsmouth, Port Vale and QPR only had to win against nothing to play for opposition, which they all duly did with ease.

QPR fans rubbed it in with style. An internet poll for the public to vote for the most influential person of the last millennium was somehow infiltrated by Rangers fans who managed to secure Jamie Pollock first place ahead of Jesus Christ! Pollock had scored an amazing own-goal against QPR that ultimately saved them at City's expense.

Martyn and Will had attended that game. The long trip up from Devon saw very little of the usual banter. We were far too nervous for that; even if we were buoyed by the news that Georgiou 'Kinky' Kinkladze would be returning from injury (and Royle's lack of trust) to face the R's. Surely the little maestro would save us?

When Kinky scored with a sublime free-kick inside the first minute, the authors and 32,000 other Blues really started to believe that it would be our day and we would be surviving at QPR's expense.

This optimism soon started to fade when inside 10 minutes City conceded a joke equaliser. Martyn Margetson (surely City's worst ever 'keeper) had picked up a back pass to concede an indirect free-kick. Instead of hanging on to the ball to buy time to organise a defensive wall, Margetson handed the ball to a QPR player who promptly squared the ball for former City striker Mike Sheron to roll the ball into an unguarded net.

Twenty odd minutes in, cue Pollock's party piece – one of the most extraordinary own-goals ever seen. Not your run of the mill deflection of a low hard cross, oh no. How about deftly flicking an opposition cross up and over two players before heading towards your own goalkeeper, only to see it fly over his head and into the net!

We did manage a Desmond (2-2) but that wasn't enough and so that is how we arrived at our lowest footballing ebb. Nationwide (nothing to do with Frank Bough) League Two it may have been by name but it was decidedly third rate. We would also suffer the ignominy of being in the Football League Trophy and the first round of the FA Cup.

City were now lower in the footballing hierarchy than North West minnows Bury, Crewe and Stockport, while next season's local derby would not be against United but against Macclesfield Town!

Was this the beginning of the end?

Embarking on Etihad Flight 2011
(Destination Promised Land)

Fast-forward 13 years and the story was somewhat different, with City unofficially the richest club in the world!

This particular leg of the journey started in Summer 2007 with manager-less City still flat broke. Us long suffering fans had just endured an appalling season under Stuart Pearce. We finished a not so bad 14th, but scored a meagre 29 goals in 38 games. This included not scoring a single goal at home from after New Year's Day right up until the end of the season!

This was a mind-numbingly boring time to be a City fan. Eight games without a single goal, and apart from two woefully missed penalties, we had never even looked like scoring.

Such was the blind faith of the authors that we went to four of the games, even recruiting Martyn's younger brother Josh to the cause. He stayed true to the faith despite witnessing being completely outplayed and defeated by the footballing giants of Reading!

The run cost Pearce his job and the foreseeable future looked pretty bleak.

Then out of the (sky) blue came a white knight in the form of former Prime Minister of Thailand, Thaksin Shinawatra. He bought out the City shareholders and promised to pump millions into the club and team.

The deal went through with Shinawatra passing the Premier League's fit and proper person test, despite the protests of Amnesty International among others, who questioned his human rights record during his term in office as Thai PM.

You just couldn't make it up. Our beloved club were now owned by somebody that was being accused in some quarters of being a despot, murderer, fraudster and embezzler!

The morals of most football fans extend no further than informing their partners 30 minutes before departure that they were off to see the match, so with promises of riches galore, who were we to question the source of the funds and Shinawatra's motives for buying City?

The club was transformed. Sven-Göran Eriksson of England, platform shoes and Ulrikakakaka fame was hired as manager, just in time to hurriedly assemble a new team that would challenge for honours.

Tens of millions were spent on a foreign legion of Brazilians Geovanni and Elano, Roland Bianchi of Italy, Vedrun Corluka, the Czech defender, Bulgarian striker Valerij Bojanov and his compatriot winger Martin Petrov. Swiss international Gelson Fernandes and Spanish defender Javier Garrido were also drafted in.

New City got off to a flyer and headed the table early doors, only to fade amid amazing rumours regarding their Thai owner, now officially in exile from Thailand, his assets frozen and facing arrest if he ever set foot in Bangkok Airport again.

Sven paid for his ultimate failure with his job, no doubt with another fat redundancy cheque to soften the blow. The last straw was a final day thrashing, 8-1 at the hands of Middlesbrough.

The authors witnessed the Boro debacle via Sky Sports updates from the same Greenwich pub where only a few weeks earlier we had watched City ruin United's 50th anniversary of the Munich air disaster commemorations by winning 2-1 at Old Trafford and thus completing a rare League double over our local rivals.

Sven was a dead man walking even before that final humiliation. Failure was not a word that Thaksin understood and he wielded the axe even though we had flukily qualified for European football by virtue of our position in the Premier League Fair Play League, together with England winning the national European version.

Shinawatra brought in Mark Hughes from Blackburn, the former United striker and ex-boss of Wales to replace Sven – a decent enough appointment we all thought.

Then IT happened. The deal that shook the football world to its core. At the start of the 2008-09 season, our beloved soap opera of a club Manchester City were bought by the Abu Dhabi royal family, who are said to be worth $500 billion.

Martyn and Will were beside themselves with excitement. The papers were suddenly full of stories of how City would dominate football and buy the best players in world football – Ronaldo, Kaka and Messi were all touted as City stars of the future.

City would win the Premier League in one, two or three years depending on who's opinion you believed. The European Champions League would follow. United would be bridesmaids and City the bride for a change.

Brazilian superstar Robinho was amazingly captured from Real Madrid on transfer deadline day at the end of August for an estimated £32.5 million (a new British record transfer fee). On the same day, City tried to hijack United's intended purchase of Bulgarian striker Dimitar Berbatov from Spurs. This late attempt failed but it pushed the purchase price that United had to pay to over £30 million.

United's legendary manager Sir Alex Ferguson was livid. Such fun. We were suddenly supporters of the most talked about club in Europe, if not the world.

City went from 'everybody's second favourite team', to being enviously disliked by the fans of most other clubs. The gallant losers were suddenly challengers. Harmless City had some teeth and the football establishment did not like it.

We were nouveau riche and brash. Loadsamoney in club form.

When the hype died down, we remained Typical City. Consistently inconsistent.

In the September Martyn and Will travelled to the Portsmouth home game from Will's South London home. We witnessed an absolute masterclass in attacking football as City demolished Pompey 6-0.

Robinho was simply sublime and his attacking interchanges with Stephen Ireland some of the best skills we had ever witnessed from City. It was champagne football, played with panache, verve, vigour, style, you name your own superlative and it will fit.

As the sixth goal crashed in, Will turned smiling to his nephew and uttered the words, 'you'd better get used to this Martyn, this is the new brand of City'.

The very next game we lost 2-1 at lowly Wigan!

The season saw City's first foray into European competition for 20 years and they did fairly well, reaching the quarter-finals before bowing out to Hamburg.

As well as Robinho, City had strengthened well in August with what were to prove to be pivotal signings in Vincent Kompany, and (Will's favourite) Pablo Zabaleta (plus returning fans favourite Shaun Wright-Phillips and £20 million flop Jo). Nigel de Jong, Shay Given, Craig Bellamy and Wayne Bridge joined them in January, as European success and automatic qualification for the Europa League via their League position was sought.

In the preliminary round we played a team from the Faroe Islands, difficult and very expensive to get to. This did not stop one group of diehards who drove to the tip of Scotland, got a ferry to the Shetlands and then hitched on a fishing trawler to the Faroes.

This summed up the type of people that follow City – resourceful, clever, a little bit crazy and always looking for a laugh.

In reaching the last eight, it seemed that City had beaten half the teams in Denmark (three in fact). Upon drawing FC Copenhagen in the knock-out stages, Will enquired of his wife, 'you have always wanted to go to Scandinavia haven't you?'

Will skilfully managed to make his European debut, while treating Mrs L to some scenic canals and a horrendously priced glass of wine.

City fans took over the city centre. European football was a shiny new toy for the vast majority of the supporters and everybody was determined to have a good time, even at €7 for a litre of beer.

The outside of pubs were bedecked in City flags and inside resonated to songs dedicated to the Blues – 'We'll drink, a drink, a drink, to Colin the King, the King, the King, he's the leader of Man City, he's the greatest, inside-forward, that the World has EVER seen.'

The match itself was played out in part during a snowstorm. City fans had to watch the game through a huge net that hung from the stand roof. We were unsure whether it was there to stop us getting on the pitch or to protect us from one of Robinho's wayward shots.

The game finished Desmond and both City goals were celebrated wildly by one particular City fan who leapt onto said net, swinging it backwards and forwards before being helped back down. He had obviously spent at least €63 on beer. Hilarious!

After the quarter-final defeat against Hamburg, the season petered out somewhat and we only managed to finish a disappointing 10th.

The end of season report officially stated that the owners were satisfied but in truth Hughes knew that we had to do a lot better in the following one.

Hughes drew up his Summer 2009 transfer target list and pulled off a major coup in obtaining the services of Carlos Tevez from United/Kia Joorabchian/South American Fruit Farmer Co-operative or whoever actually owned him.

The fact was that he had been playing for United for the past two seasons and was well liked by their fans who sang his name and urged Fergie (Alex Ferguson) to sign him up.

Fergie declined, or dithered at least and City swooped. His arrival was greeted with fervour by the authors and all City fans, while United fans were dismayed.

During all the years of United dominance and City mediocrity, the one thing that used to upset the Reds, was the fact that City are officially Manchester's only club as United are based in the satellite city of Salford. This meant that United could not have the Manchester coat of arms on their club badge.

A very small irritant you would think when compared to countless trophies and titles but this seemingly trivial fact really gets up United noses.

The City humorists could not resist a dig when Tevez signed and somebody (nobody will admit who) paid for a huge billboard to be erected in Manchester city centre with a picture of Tevez above the words 'welcome to Manchester'.

This really hit the mark with Fergie accusing us of being small-minded, disrespectful and calling us 'the Noisy Neighbours'. The poster had really rattled him and many connected with the Salford club. They hated having a challenge from a supposed non-entity club on their doorstep. We were becoming a force to be reckoned with.

That close season England regular Gareth Barry arrived from Aston Villa, centre-back Joleon Lescott from Everton together with Arsenal pair Emanuel Adebayor and Kolo Toure. Together the acquisitions cost about £100 million. A far cry from 1998 when we barely spent £100,000.

For the authors and all of our fellow Blues, this was fantasy football. Star players suddenly prefering City to ply their trade ahead of traditional Giants of the game like United, Liverpool and Arsenal. Sure, generous wages were a factor but equally as important was the City Blueprint, the vision that had City dominating England and eventually Europe.

With decent wages secure pretty much wherever they play, it is playing success that the top players really crave.

The season started well enough with City staying in the top few for the first few months of the season. We had in fact won our first four games before facing United at Old Trafford.

Will watched an amazing game unfold while in Greece, having found a Central Athens bar showing the game. Well in fact half the game. The locals wanted to watch a nondescript Greek game played in front of a few hundred people on a cabbage patch of a pitch so the bar owner tried to please everybody by alternating 10 minutes from Old Trafford and then 10 minutes from Old Decrepit Park.

So we had 10 minutes showing some of the finest players in world football, playing in front of 75,000 vocal supporters, in one of the finest stadiums in the world, in one of football's greatest local derbies, followed by 10 minutes of third rate football, in a third rate stadium, played by a bunch of nobodies in front of a few friends and family!

The fact that the Manchester derby threw up a feast of football with some stunning goals just made matters worse. To add insult to injury (time), the TV switched over to the Greek Garbage with three minutes of extra (Fergie) time remaining.

Will had assumed the game had finished 3-3, with City heroically equalising three times, the last being a 90th minute special from Craig Bellamy. That was until he received a text from Martyn which simply read 'F**K!'

The five minutes of injury time had somehow extended to eight minutes with United scoring a winner in the 96th minute.

As 44-year-old's strops go, this took some beating. Name any expletive you want before the word cheats and you get the picture. Will's Greek friends didn't know where to look. Suddenly they were apparently very interested in the cabbage patch game that was now being shown uninterrupted.

City went downhill after this match and went on a record breaking run of seven consecutive draws to effectively put them out of contention for the title. Will had taken nephew Josh to a seemingly easy home game against Burnley during this run but it finished 3-3, so Josh was still yet to see City win in Manchester.

In the middle of December City travelled to Spurs for a midweek game. The best City could realistically hope for at this stage was Champions League qualification by merit of finishing in the top four of the Premier League.

Spurs were one of City's main rivals for a fourth place finish, so the game was billed as a proverbial six pointer.

Will paid his £55 to see if City could break their White Hart Lane hoodoo but his beloved team just didn't turn up that night. In fact we pretty much played the game with nine men with Robinho and Adebayor seemingly on strike and refusing to get any sweat on their pristine shirts. Spurs won 3-0 at a canter.

This did grave damage to Mark Hughes' City career. The power brokers at the club met and agreed that Hughes had to go. He had always been the appointment of the former regime and now he had lost the dressing room and the confidence of the fans. We wanted Hughes out.

City handled his sacking badly. We were beating Sunderland 4-3 at home when the news broke. You had the unsavoury sight of Hughes watching the game unfold from the touchline with everybody including Hughes and his management team knowing that the game was up for them.

The unwanted Christmas present was duly presented to Hughes and his coaches – their P45s.

So who would take over? The smart money was on former Inter Milan boss Roberto Mancini, who was out of work and very available. It was safe to say that he wasn't a universally popular choice. We wanted Jose Mourinho.

Bobby Manc as he affectionately became known, duly took over for the second half of the season with a clear brief – get City into the Champions League this season.

Results improved and sufficiently to have us challenging for fourth place. We also had a two legged semi-final against United in the League Cup.

Up until the semi, United had played a second string team in every round. Not against City.

Will went to the first leg at The City of Manchester Stadium to hear a full strength United team named. They were determined to stop City winning any silverware so that their fans could keep unfurling the 34 years banner, symbolising the 34 years since City had won a major trophy.

The atmosphere was electric and the pace of the game frenetic. United took the lead early on but by half-time City were 2-1 up, both goals coming from Tevez, who promptly wound up Fergie and United's loathsome substitute right-back Gary Neville by celebrating his second goal enthusiastically right in front of them.

'Fergie, Fergie, sign him up,' the City fans mocked in reference to United fans' chants towards the end of the previous season.

Will travelled back to London by train the next day. As he sat at his seat, about to do some work, he heard what he thought to be Italian voices. He looked up just to see a group of casually stylish men walking down the aisle in his direction.

They were indeed Italians (they would have to be either gay or Italian to be stylishly casual!), and in fact it were none other than Roberto Mancini, goalkeeping coach Massimo Battara and a couple of others.

Will's inner child got the better of him. He had to go and speak with Roberto. His wife who fancied him rotten would be extremely envious!

Wait until they are settled, have a coffee, get past Stoke and then go for it. Off Will trotted and soon found himself face to face with the great man. 'Roberto, could I have a photo with you?' Will meekly whispered. How embarrassing, he was only on the phone!

Roberto was only too willing to oblige, despite Will's imperfect timing. He put down the phone and Will handed his blackberry to one of his entourage. 'Well done on last night's result, hope we finish them off in the second leg,' was all that Will could muster by way of conversation – after all Roberto had a phone call to go back to.

Mancini politely thanked Will who returned to his seat like a kid in a sweet shop.

United had the last laugh this time by virtue of a second leg 3-1 win to go through 4-3 on aggregate. Another injury time winner naturally. 34 years was to turn into 35.

The season ultimately came down to one game. City at home to Spurs, with the winner virtually guaranteed fourth place and Champions League qualification.

The match was billed as winner takes all. Spurs had become one of City's bogie teams (Everton were the other), so it was with nervous excitement and hope the fans approached the game rather than expectation.

Will had been to the match two games prior with younger nephew Josh (Jonah!), a 1-0 home defeat against United (at least their 89th minute winner was in normal time on this occasion). City had been very negative in that game, trying for a precious point in their pursuit of fourth spot.

Mancini had started to favour a cautious approach. This was just not the City way. The team was stacked with flair players like Bellamy, Adebayor, Tevez, Adam Johnson and Wright-Phillips, as well as flying full-backs Micah Richards and Pablo Zabaleta. Spurs completely outplayed us and deservedly won 1-0 through a late Peter Crouch goal. It was to be Thursday nights on Channel Five for us again in the Europa League.

Mancini had not met his goal but had done enough to suggest better times were ahead. He was entrusted with the Petrol Dollar kitty to strengthen the squad still further. And boy did he spend!

Yaya Toure from Barcelona, David Silva from Valencia, Mario Balotelli from Inter Milan, James Milner from Aston Villa. Again over £100 million.

This finally did the trick. We pretty much stayed in the top four all season and in April we found ourselves in the FA Cup semi-final against United at Wembley.

The authors procured tickets and proudly took their place behind the goal. City fans got to the ground early for our biggest Wembley cup game for many a year.

Will had attended the last 'big' cup game there involving City, the 1986 Full Members Cup Final. A second rate tournament contrived by City and FA chairman Peter Swales. City lost that one 5-4 against Chelsea with David Speedie scoring the first Wembley hat-trick since Sir Geoff.

This was new ground for the vast majority of us and we wanted to enjoy the occasion. The United part of the ground was virtually empty. This was standard fare for them and nothing to get too excited about.

For us this was BIG! We wanted to win so badly. It was one of those games that you absolutely sang your heart out. 'BLUE MOON, YOU SAW ME STANDING ALONE, WITHOUT A DREAM IN MY HEART, WITHOUT A LOVE OF MY OWN.'

United battered us for 25 minutes as the goal that stood right in front of us led a charmed life. Berbatov somehow contrived to miss from three yards out when faced with an open goal.

Slowly but surely, City wrestled the advantage their way with Enfant Terrible Mario Balotelli (he had already been sent off twice in his short City career and seemed to court controversy wherever he went on and off the pitch) having a controlled and very effective game.

City started to dominate and could easily have reached half-time in front. The domination continued into the second half and then in the 52nd minute, right in front of the massed City hordes, Yaya Toure scored what was to prove to be the winner.

The celebrations were wild when the ball hit the back of the net. A massed, heaving love-in followed by an energetic version of the Poznan (all City fans turn their back on the pitch and the opposing fans, link arms and bounce up and down while singing, 'Let's all do the Poznan, let's all do the Poznan, La La La La, La La La La'). City may have copied this from Europa League opponents Lech Poznan but had adopted this as their own and at least gave deference to their new Polish friends by christening it the Poznan.

There was no way back for United, Arch villain and United legend Paul Scholes was sent off and that was that. Super Mario (Balotelli) endeared himself at the end to us City fans by taunting Rio Ferdinand, the United and England centre-back, causing him to lose his temper. They don't like it up 'em Captain Mainwaring!

As the City fans celebrated wildly and Will gave Martyn an enormous bear-hug, the entire City team came over and did an enthusiastic rendition of the Poznan in front of us. Absolute class. The team may be highly paid and cosseted, but there seemed to be a real affinity developing.

The semi-final win galvanised City who had been inconsistent of late and had slipped to fourth place in the League, with Champions League qualification in the balance.

Unbelievably a May midweek home fixture with Spurs was again crucial. If City won they would be guaranteed fourth spot and qualification, if we lost Spurs would only be three points behind with two games to play.

We had seen it all before, Spurs were a bogie side who pipped us the previous year and had a history of beating us in the Cup Final, quarter-finals and of course the League. We were not confident.

The 2010 nemesis Peter Crouch again scored the winner – only this time it was an own goal!

This secured City a spot in the premier European competition for the first time ever. We had again reached the Europa League quarter-final (losing to Dynamo Kiev) but the Champions League was where it was at – City were finally there!

Having endured 90 minutes of sheer tension, Martyn and Will were now free to exchange texts on whether we would be playing Barcelona at the Camp Nou or Real Madrid at the Bernebeau. This really was a dream come true!

Next up the Cup Final against Stoke City, four days later. Bizarrely, this was to be played at the same time as normal League fixtures. The FA Cup is THE domestic cup, the most famous in the world and well over 100 years old (City had in fact played and lost in the Centenary Final way back in 1981) but the FA had messed around with it over recent years to diminish its status slightly.

Anyway, the Final was still of vital importance to City, even more so for us fans that had endured 35 years of hurt since their previous meaningful Cup win, the 1976 League Cup triumph, which had also been played on a Saturday around normal League fixtures – was this a good omen?

The authors and Josh, watched the game at Will's home. We could have had a ticket for about £200 each but would have been in different parts of Wembley and wanted to experience the match within hugging distance of each other.

We had our own special homemade build up.

City flags adorned the front of the house, Will's dog Oli sported sky blue and white ribbons, Martyn slaughtered Josh in the Will prepared City Mastermind, we each had a copy of the official programme purchased from WH Smith and ate steak pudding, chips and gravy for lunch (a Manchester delicacy; many times in the past, dour games at Maine Road had been brightened by this calorific meal from the City Chippy on Claremont Road, washed down with pints of Boddingtons at the Bee Hive).

Blue Moon lager was the choice of beverage for the day.

(Manchester) City pretty much dominated the whole game but it seemed would never score. We really feared that Stoke would send one of their infamous long balls into the box, which would lead to a scramble, followed by a miss hit shot being deflected in!

At least that is what the otherwise optimistic Will thought (backed up by his 'never optimistic about City' mate Burfield, who agreed via text from his Wembley seat). Martyn and Josh just thought it was a matter of time.

The young ones were right, thankfully. City finally scored to earn a single goal victory via a 74th minute strike from semi-final hero Yaya Toure.

The house erupted! Cheers, Hugs, Kisses, Lounge Lap of Honour, Dancing with the Dog and teetotal Martyn even had a sip of champagne!

This was absolutely brilliant. We had not even come close to winning any top honours in Martyn's lifetime, Will could barely remember the 1976 victory, while Josh was a little nonplussed by it all as he had only endured about six years of relative hurt, all of which had been in the Premier League at least.

Captain King Carlos lifted the trophy aloft and a suburban home erupted once more, 'Carlos Tevez is a Blue, is a Blue, is a Blue!'

At last, the City mirror Will got from his parents for Christmas 1976 was no longer in date!

And things were to get even better. City won their final two League games (including Stoke at home three days after the Cup Final, classily City foregoing the opportunity to show the Cup off to their fans and therefore rubbing Stoke noses in it), while third place Arsenal faltered.

This meant that City finished third (easily their highest ever Premier League finish), and therefore had qualified straight into the Champions League group stages rather than facing a potentially tricky preliminary round Play-off.

Let the good times roll…

City Expects

City found themselves as favourites in many quarters to win the League.

That's about as close a comparison that you can draw between 1998-99 season and 2011-12.

The fall-out from the 1998 relegation had been palpable. Never before in City's 118-year history had they ever played third-tier football. Doom mongers of the press wrote that this could be the end of Manchester City, that we may never regain top-flight status.

Flat broke and having lost their only stars (Kinky signed for Ajax for £5 million and Uwe Rosler left on a free transfer), there were plenty of doubters out there that claimed City would struggle to get out of this tough division, full of uncompromising defenders, long ball tactics and tiny grounds.

Every time City travelled to play against one of the plentiful minnows that they would be up against, it would be a Cup Final for the home team and their fans. They would rise to the occasion and make life extremely difficult.

The one thing that City had that was top class was the fans. We had averaged over 28,000 per match in the previous disastrous season (topped by a crowd of over 32,000 for the calamitous QPR game).

We remained optimistic. We would storm the League with record points and record goal difference.

In 2011 we were also optimistic. We had won the Cup and qualified for the Champions League. We had a team full of super stars, topped by Carlos Tevez, English top flight football's top scorer of the past two seasons with 52 goals and joint holder (with Berbatov) of the Premier League Golden Boot Trophy for being 2010-11 season top scorer.

Just when you thought riding the crest of a wave was without hazards, Tevez promptly asked for a transfer citing homesickness. This was to become quite a saga but the uncertainty with Tevez spurred Mancini into signing Tevez's Argentine compatriot Sergio 'Kun' Agüero from Athletico Madrid for £35 million.

Other signings that summer were Samir Nasri (£25 million) and Gael Clichy (£7 million) from Arsenal, Stefan Savic, the Montenegrin defender for £7 million and Costel Pantilimon, the giant Romanian international goalkeeper signed on loan as cover for first choice for City and England, Joe Hart.

An already strong squad had been further strengthened. We pretty much had a choice of two international players for every position. We even had the luxury of loaning out or giving away stars such as Adebayor, Bellamy, Santa Cruz, Wright-Phillips, Vladimir Weiss, John Guidetti and Dedryk Boyata – internationals one and all.

Back in '98, the close season wheeling and dealing was somewhat different.

Kinky and Uwe were joined on the exit list by such City luminaries (NOT!) as Barry Conlon, Martyn Margetson, Kit Symons, Nigel Clough, Martin Phillips, Gerry Creaney and Eddie McGoldrick.

Veteran Ian Brightwell left for Coventry with our heartfelt gratitude for all he had contributed down the years in the City cause.

With the deadwood out of the way, who would their replacements be? A player that was to become something of a City cult hero – Aussie Danny

Tiatto from Swiss football for £300,000 and fellow Aussie Danny Allsopp for nowt. That was it!

Surely we still had the class to dominate this League, right? Joe Royle had re-signed former City favourite Ian Bishop (one of Will's all time City idols) and prolific lower League goalscorer Shaun Goater towards the end of the 1997-98 season as part of our failed survival attempt and much of our hopes rested on these two players.

We also had the likes of Paul Dickov, Kevin Horlock, Richard Edghill, Nicky Weaver, the unfortunate Jamie Pollock, Gerard Wiekens, Michael Brown and record £3 million signing Lee Bradbury (remove the r's to show what we thought of him!).

City were the bookies favourites for the title, with their main rivals thought to be current Premier League clubs Fulham, Wigan, Reading and Stoke, with Gillingham down as dark horses.

Talking of Premier League, 2011 City were also among the favourites for the title. Arch rivals and defending champions United were the ones to beat, with the London trio of Chelsea, Arsenal and Spurs the other main fancies.

City had the players, they had the momentum from the previous season and most pundits believed they had the management team. The only thing missing was the experience of actually winning the top League.

The Toure brothers had done it (Kolo at Arsenal and Yaya at Barca), Kompany had won the Belgian League twice at Anderlecht, Edin Džeko the Bundesliga for Wolfsburg and Tevez and Clichy had been Premier League winners with United and Arsenal respectively.

On the management side, Mancini won the Scudetto in Italy three times at Internazionale, Brian Kidd was coach at United when they first won the PL, Patrick Vieira was part of Arsenals 'invincibles' team that won the League without losing a game and coach David Platt had also won the title at Arsenal as a player.

Despite this, the team had never done it, no matter how good they were individually; did they have the mental strength to get over the line as a group?

While pre-season games are basically there for players to hone their fitness, to bed in new signings and try out new tactics, fans tend to hold them up as a sign of things to come. A successful pre-season augers well, while a dodgy run of friendly results is seen as a portent of doom. This rarely materialises as the case, but we still fall for it every year.

In 2011 pre-season would be an international tournament in Dublin featuring Celtic and Inter Milan, high profile Stateside matches against MLS opposition including David Beckham's LA Galaxy and the Community Shield against United at Wembley.

The class of '98 headed to Cornwall. Joe Royle was a well-known advocate of having extremely fit players, favouring the 'get stuck in' brand of football.

The City squad therefore headed for the Naval training base in Torpoint on the River Tamar for some military style fitness drills. Friendlies were arranged against Cornish minnows Torpoint Athletic and Newquay.

Being West Country boys and members of the South West Supporters Club, we headed for the Torpoint game, the attraction being not so much the game as the chance to meet the players afterwards in the social club.

We barely actually left the social club as it absolutely chucked it down so that the game was a muddy farce. If memory serves Will well, he thinks it ended 2-2 but the result was pretty meaningless. Royle was pleased to have seen his players rise to the challenge in atrocious conditions – he reckoned he had some battlers in the team and that is what he liked.

After the game, a chance to meet the team and management. City may have been third tier, but to the authors they were still demi-gods. Martyn was amazed to be in the same room as Shaun Goater and Kevin Horlock, while Will was amazed at just how big Joe Royle's head was!

Then the pièce de résistence. A sports quiz. Teams of four were hurriedly assembled. The players divided themselves into fours, as did the fans. That's all except for the authors who formed an under-strength team with City's dutch centre-half Gerard Wiekens.

The triumvirate soon forged into an early lead. We were sat next to a team made up of Ian Bishop, Paul Dickov, Lee Bradbury and Michael Brown who soon realised that we were the team to beat.

They proceeded to try and look at our answer sheet and offered bribes for revealing the correct answers.

We refused to buckle, even as Brown's language got choicer and choicer!

Name the six racecourses in the UK that begin with the letter W*. Thirty seconds later, we had them all written down. They could only get five. 'Come on you bastards, what's the sixth?' implored Brown. 'Not telling', replied Martyn smugly.

We romped home and Martyn went up to collect the winning champers to a chorus of, 'Statto!, Statto!, Statto!' (Statto was the name given to football fact meister Angus Loughran on *Fantasy Football League*, an extremely popular Friday night footie programme of the time, presented by Frank Skinner and David Baddiel on BBC2).

Wiekens signed the champagne box and punch drunk on our victory success, we vowed to open the bottle if City got back to the Premier in two years. 'We will try,' responded Gerard, more in hope than expectation...

In 2011 it was winning the Premier League that was the goal. Pre-season had gone well with City unbeaten until they faced Champions United in the traditional season curtain raiser at Wembley.

Agüero wasn't fit enough to start, while Tevez had 'leave of absence' to remain in Argentina.

City did not play at all well but against the run of play they raced into a two-goal lead thanks to Džeko and Lescott (plus a helping hand from nervous new United goalkeeper De Gea).

United turned it around completely in the second half and ran out deserved 3-2 winners. The season's first medals had gone to the tried and trusted champs. Fuel for all the City doubters.

Martyn and Will exchanged texts and agreed that, 'we would rather lose this "friendly" than a League game against them'. We were yet to unleash our Argentinian strike force and we expected Nasri to be on board soon. No worries.

Reds striker Wayne Rooney tweeted, 'we taught City a footballing lesson today'. Let's see if we were good learners...

* For the record they are Warwick, Wetherby, Wincanton, Windsor, Wolverhampton and Worcester.

Meet the Teams

Goalkeeper 1998

Nicky Weaver – signed as a promising youngster from Mansfield Town and now first choice at 20 years old.

Goalkeeper 2011

Joe Hart – signed as a promising youngster from Shrewsbury Town and first choice for City and England. 25 years old. Our best 'keeper since Bert Trautman.

Right-back 1998

Lee Crooks – 21-year-old product of the youth squad with little first-team experience. Hard as nails and already a fans' favourite.

Right-back 2011

Micah Richards – product of the youth academy and England's youngest ever full international defender when aged 18. Now 24 with 12 full caps. Would run through a wall in City's cause, the fans love his cavalier approach to football, even if he does give us palpitations at times.

Left-back 1998

Richard Edghill – another product of the youth squad, often the victim of abuse from the terraces, unfairly thought the authors. Aged 24 and had appeared for England at Under-21 and B level.

Left-back 2011

Gael Clichy – just signed from Arsenal for £7 million. Twenty-six-year-old full international for France and Premier League medal holder. A decent defender who also is effective in attack.

Centre-backs 1998

Gerard Wiekens – 26-year-old signed from Dutch football in '97. Can also operate in midfield. An assured, skilful if unspectacular player. We trusted him.

Tony Vaughan – 22-year-old who cost £1.35 million from Ipswich who could also play full-back. Struggling to live up to price tag. Average.

Centre-backs 2011

Vincent Kompany – the new club captain, 26-year-old Belgian international signed for a bargain £6 million in 2008 from Hamburg. We love him!

Joleon Lescott – signed for a remarkable £22 million from Everton in 2010. England international now finding his feet at City after a shaky start.

Midfielders 1998

Ian Bishop – signed in spring '97 for a second spell with City. Classy midfielder but at 34 past his best.

Jamie Pollock – had been signed in March '98 for a cool £1 million from Bolton and tasked with keeping City up. Instead scored a calamitous own-goal that condemned City to relegation. 24-year-old with 200 first-team appearances to his name. He owed us one!

Kevin Horlock – Frank Clark's first signing when City paid £1.25 million for the Northern Ireland international in 1997. Now 25. Already had an affinity with the fans who enjoyed his vision, passing ability and battling qualities.

Michael Brown – came through the ranks at City. The 22-year-old was already known as a tough tackling midfielder, actually being sent off on his debut for two bad tackles having come on as sub only 10 minutes beforehand (as witnessed by Will in August 95). England Under-21 international.

Midfielders 2011

Gareth Barry – England regular signed for £12 million from Aston Villa in 2010. Aged 30. Mr Dependable – the sort of player every flair team needs.

Yaya Toure – 28-year-old Ivory Coast international who cost £24 million from Barcelona in 2010 and had won every domestic, European and World honour with the Spanish giants. A giant in every way and a bulldozer of a player.

David Silva – Spanish international signed from Valencia in 2010. The 25-year-old is both a World Cup and European Championship winner for his country. Known to City fans as Merlin due to him being a magician with the ball!

Samir Nasri – prised away from Arsenal just after the season started for £25 million. A very talented French wide player. Over 20 caps for his country and only aged 24. He had chosen City over United so had already endeared himself to the City faithful before a ball was kicked.

Strikers 1998

Shaun Goater – former United apprentice with 113 goals in 288 lower League appearances for Rotherham and Bristol City. Signed by Royle with seven games remaining in the previous season, his three goals were not enough to save City. Aged 28, a lot of City hopes rested on his shoulders. Bermuda international.

Paul Dickov – a £1 million signing from Arsenal in August 1996 and had been City's top scorer with nine goals during the last fateful season. Known more for his phenomenal work rate than his scoring exploits, 25-year-old 'Dicky' was a favourite of the fans (including the authors). Scotland Under-21 international.

Lee Bradbury – Lee Badbuy as he was unaffectionately known, had cost a club record fee of £3 million when he signed from Portsmouth in July 1997. With the price tag weighing heavily, he had contributed just six goals in his first season. Aged 23. The fans expected him to be prolific at this level.

Danny Allsopp – came initially on trial from Australian football, and taken on by Joe Royle after scoring in the Newquay friendly as a 19-year-old. Australia Under-20 cap. A rookie with potential.

Strikers 2011

Edin Džeko – 25-year-old Bosnian international signed from Wolfsburg for £28 million in the January transfer window. Prolific in German football with 66 goals in 111 games. After a slow City start, a lot was expected of the 6ft 4in striker in the new season.

Sergio Agüero – 23-year-old Argentine international and the son-in-law of legendary Diego Maradona, Kun broke City's transfer record, costing £35 million from Athletico Madrid in July. He had scored 101 goals in 234 games in Spain, while also contributing an impressive 37 assists. He won the Europa League while in Madrid and was an Olympic Gold medallist for Argentina. City fans were more excited about this signing than perhaps any other in recent history.

Carlos Tevez – 52 goals in two seasons, the first City captain to lift a major trophy aloft in 35 years and a player who openly dislikes former club Manchester United and Sir Alex. All the ingredients to become a true City legend. Cue bombshell. He is homesick and wants to leave. Stripped of the captaincy but still on the City books as the season starts, but for how long? 27-year-old with over 50 caps for Argentina.

Mario Balotelli – the 20-year-old Italian international joined City in August 2010 from Inter Milan, for whom he had played under Mancini. The whole book could be filled with Mario stories, suffice to say he is controversial both on and off the pitch! A fantastic player on his day, but could he be trusted? Italy's first ever black international.

Manager 1998

Joe Royle – as a player for City, he was a part of the last all-star City team of the mid '70s. When City won their last major trophy, the 1976 League Cup, Royle had scored in every round bar the Final. An England international, Royle also had a successful playing career with Everton, Bristol City and Norwich. As a manager, he had earned his reputation at Oldham, taking an unfashionable club into the Premier League and to the Final of the League Cup. Royle also won the FA Cup while manager of Everton and took over at City in February '98, eight years after turning the City job down while at Oldham.

Manager 2011

Roberto Mancini – a decorated player in Italian football with League and Cup and European club honours with Sampdoria and Lazio as well as 36 full international caps. He got his first taste of English football as a player for Leicester for whom he played four times on loan from Lazio in 2001. As a manager he had won the Italian title three times and the Italian cup twice with Internazionale before taking over at City in December 2010 and taking them to their first major trophy in 35 years in last season's FA Cup. Already a legend therefore and also with City's first ever Champions League qualification on his CV.

In Reserve 1998

Tommy Wright – Goalkeeper, veteran Northern Ireland international stopper.

Murtaz Shelia – Full-back, injury stricken Georgian international.

Kakhaber Tskhadze – Centre-back, same as Murtaz Shelia.

Nick Fenton – Centre-back, young defender who had come up through the City ranks.

Jim Whitley – Midfield, decidedly average central midfielder.

Jeff Whitley – Midfield, younger and more talented brother of Jim.

Gary Mason – Midfield, promising 18-year-old Scot.

Danny Tiatto – Midfield/Full-back – our 'big' summer signing, 25-year-old Aussie cap.

Craig Russell – Forward – 24-year-old signed November '97 in swap deal, valued at £1 million. How?

In Reserve 2011

Costel Pantilimon – Goalkeeper, Romanian international brought in on loan as cover.

Pablo Zabaleta – Full-back, Will's favourite City player. Never say die Argentine cap.

Aleksander Kolarov – Left-back, 25-year-old Serb international with blistering shot.

Kolo Toure – Centre-back, older brother of Yaya. Very good Ivory Coast international.

Stefan Savic – Centre-back, young Montenegrin, one for the future.

Nigel de Jong – Midfield, Dutch enforcer and real fans' favourite, arrived January 2009.

James Milner – Midfield, £21 million signing from Aston Villa. England cap and great squad player.

Adam Johnson – Winger, joined for £6 million in January 2010. England cap and super-sub.

Squad of 1998

Assembled for around £10 million, massive for third tier standards. Six full internationals for minor footballing nations but predominantly undecorated players. Seven homegrown players.

Squad of 2011

Assembled for well over £300 million, massive by any standards. Every player a full international and between them had already won virtually every honour in football. One homegrown player (pinched from Oldham's academy!).

2

LET BATTLE COMMENCE

The First Halves

Now it was for real, 8 August 1998 and City were in new territory. A North West derby against Blackpool at Maine Road. Over 32,000 crammed into the ground that had hosted Premier League football just three years previously.

The stadium was the same (four completely individual stands) but the backdrop to the game was very different. Will and Martyn listened on the radio and like the majority in the ground that day, expected – no demanded – a comfortable City victory.

We were not disappointed. 3-0 to the Sky Blues with goals from Goater, Bradbury and the unpronounceable Georgian. This season was going to be easy. We would win the League at a canter.

2011 started in similar fashion with a resounding 4-0 victory against Swansea. Most excitingly for the 47,000 in the newly christened Etihad Stadium and the fans, like the authors, that watched on television was the unleashing of Sergio Agüero.

Brought on after an hour with the score at 1-0, he scored a debut goal after eight minutes, laid on another for Silva three minutes later, before scoring a belter in injury time to cap the victory.

The authors were beside themselves. Will likened him to Torres before his injury. Perhaps the most explosive debut in Premier League history. If he could do that in half an hour, what could he do in the full 90 minutes? Scores of texts passed between the authors. 'City are the real deal', 'get your money on City for the title and Kun for the Golden Boot', 'quake in your boots Fergie!'

City were less convincing in their next game, a 3-2 win at Bolton, before they travelled to White Hart Lane. City had just one point from their previous seven visits. Will had suffered four consecutive 2-1 defeats and the 3-0 drubbing in 2009 on his most recent visits to Spurs' ground, so on taking his standing place at the Lane (all seater of course but nobody sat for the entire game), he was feeling pretty nervous.

After the opening exchanges were fairly even (and in fairness Spurs had the best of the chances), City broke away after 34 minutes to score through Džeko. He did it again five minutes later to put us two up. 'Blue Moon etc, etc', 'let's all do the Poznan', the City fans went wild in the August sunshine.

In the second half, Kun got a third, Džeko completed his hat-trick to put us four up before Kaboul pulled one back. Then in stoppage time, dream land. Džeko picked the ball up outside the area before unleashing an unstoppable shot that arrowed into the left-hand corner of the net. Five bloody one!!

Will hugged the Geordie Blue next to him. After years of suffering at Tottenham, Will had just witnessed City's biggest ever win at The Lane.

Texts were sent without reply to Will's five Spurs supporting colleagues. Martyn and Josh responded to theirs with delight. City were top of the table after three games and had scored 12 goals!

Will got home just in time to watch the last half hour of United v Arsenal. United needed to win by six goals and score at least seven to top City. No way! Yes way – they won 8-2!

'Manchester 13 North London 3', proclaimed the headlines. City were fantastic but United would fight them all the way. That much seemed certain already.

Back in 1998 the bright start could not be sustained in the same way. A thumping 3-0 loss at Kevin Keegan's Fulham was followed by a dire 0-0 draw at home to unfancied Wrexham and an uninspiring 1-1 draw at Notts County and that only due to Goater's 90th minute equaliser.

At the end of August City had just five points out of 12 and sat 14th in the embryonic table. The fans were underwhelmed. This was not what we had expected. 'Keep the faith,' Will implored Martyn. It was very difficult when all your schoolmates support United and Liverpool or (worse still for a youngster living in Hampshire) Southampton and Portsmouth, who were both playing at a higher level than City. Things improved in September with three consecutive wins followed by three draws on the bounce. The last of these draws had given Will a taste of the bad old days of football violence.

Recently moved to London and just three days after the move to the capital, City travelled to Millwall for a mid-week fixture.

'No one likes us, we don't care,' sang the South Londoners. No we flaming well don't! The atmosphere turned nasty in the second half. Millwall went one up in the 46th minute to send the locals delirious before a player from each side was sent off for scrapping after an hour.

Most of the players squared up to each other and perhaps more should have gone for an early bath. 'You Dirty Northern Bastards,' rang out from the home terraces. Things got worse when Millwall scored a second. There was bedlam in all but the away stand.

In all the commotion and despondency in our end, nobody seemed to notice the linesman's flag. Certainly the homies didn't as they continued to celebrate wildly. After consultation between referee and linesman, the goal was chalked off, not a clue why.

The Millwall 'supporters' went mad, 'who's the Bastard in the Black!?' If they were incensed then, they were apoplectic went Bradbury equalised in the 90th minute. 'You're going home in a fu**ing ambulance,' they collectively promised the City diehards.

We held our breath as Bradbury broke clear in injury time. We wanted him to score a winner of course but deep down were concerned that the ambulance pronouncement may well be true if he did!

We were not too upset when he found the side netting and the final whistle went soon afterwards.

After proclaiming our battling heroes who had just won a hard fought point, we turned to leave. An hour later and we were still in the ground, kept behind for our own safety.

We read reports next day of running battles between Millwall fans and police. The cockney rebels wanted to get their hands on us but frustrated in this quest, they turned on the next best thing, The Law.

Finally, some time after 11pm we were allowed out. It would be bad enough for Will to get back to Leyton but the majority of the City fans had a five-hour journey ahead of them.

As the police escorted us back to Bermondsey Station, the battleground was there for all to see. Upended trees, smashed car windscreens, bricks, bottles and other debris. A few Lion neanderthals hurled abuse and the odd stone in our direction.

One wrinkled old lady viewed the scene of carnage from her open upstairs window. 'What must she think about this chaos?' Will thought. 'Fack Off Back To Ya Northern Shi*hole,' was apparently what was on her mind – charming! City were up to seventh by the way.

Team	P	W	D	L	F	A	GS	PTS
Stoke City	10	8	0	2	17	8	17	24
Preston North End	10	6	3	1	22	11	22	21
Fulham	10	6	3	1	14	6	14	21
Blackpool	10	6	2	2	15	12	15	20
Bournemouth	10	6	2	2	14	6	14	20
Walsall	10	6	1	3	14	12	14	19
Manchester City	10	4	5	1	14	10	14	17
Luton Town	10	5	2	3	11	8	11	17

Over to 2011 post summer riot England (Spurs' first home game had been called off due to rioting and looting in Tottenham following a death of a man – scenes that were to be copied throughout the country), September saw two further City wins and their first dropped points with a Desmond at Fulham.

Will had frantically kept up to date with this match whenever Ukrainian mobile networks allowed. The BBC mobile site actually showed that City had won 3-2 but for some reason included Vinnie's own-goal both for and against us. Not since the days of Grandstand's teleprinter had such a mistake occurred that was to wipe the smile off Will's face.

Kun scored a brace in that game to put City 2 up, his 8th goal in the first 5 games to put him level with Big Micky Quinn of Coventry as the most prolific in Premier League history after five games (Quinn got a brace in his next game whilst Kun failed to score against Everton, so it is Jailbird Micky that holds the ultimate Premier League debut scoring-run record!)

The month also saw City's much-anticipated Champions League debut against Napoli. The hairs stood up on the back of Will's neck as he watched from his seat in the East Stand as the Champions League anthem reverberated around the Etihad.

He had attended ties at Anfield, Highbury, The Emirates, Stamford Bridge, San Siro and Bernebau in the past but if the truth be known, had only ever dared to dream of that music ever being played at City.

The dream had become reality and had only taken the best part of £1 billion to achieve it! Whatever the circumstances, this was still our City, the same club that had been down to the third tier of English football as little as 12 years before.

Napoli really gave City a European lesson that night, counter-attacking with verve, speed and purpose. City escaped with a 1-1 draw thanks to a Kolarov rocket but we now knew what a hard challenge lay ahead. We were in the toughest group with Bayern Munich and Villareal also our opponents, progression would not be easy.

At the end of month, City lost 2-0 in Munich to further confirm the task ahead. Will had watched the game in an Irish Bar in the Ukrainian city of Lviv, complete with German commentary. We had started the tie well but were overrun as the game wore on.

This match was to be infamous to City for more than just a resounding defeat. Carlos Tevez had gone from hero to zero in our eyes, after allegedly refusing to warm up as a substitute after Mancini's instructions to do so.

In the immediate aftermath of the game, Mancini vowed that Tevez would never play for City again. Emotions were running very high.

Will would have been totally oblivious to this (not due to four pints of Guinness but down to not understanding the German commentary) had it not been for texts from Martyn. The flavour was something like 'that Argentinian git can just f**k off home!'

The reasons for such acerbic language were then explained and Will (like most City fans) concurred with that sentiment. We simply had to back Mancini in the row.

The club duly suspended Tevez as claims and counter-claims were publicly traded. Tevez was to go AWOL, heading back to Argentina claiming he was suffering from stress and anxiety and had been treated like a dog by Mancini.

The media absolutely loved it. Most City fans share a distrust of certain sections of the press; thought to be sycophantic United fans in disguise first and impartial reporters second.

Headlines such as 'Mancini Blows it', and 'Carlos Row Threatens To Derail City Title Bid'.

City were determined to stay focused. This did seem to be a new style City, one that would not wilt under pressure and would let their play on the pitch do the talking.

Captain Courageous Vinny Kompany rallied the troops and Blackburn and Villa were duly despatched 8-1 on aggregate in early October to put City two clear of United and three ahead of Chelsea. United would be tough to shift.

Team	P	W	D	L	F	A	GD	PTS
Manchester City	8	7	1	0	27	6	21	22
Manchester United	8	6	2	0	25	6	19	20
Chelsea	8	6	1	1	20	9	11	19
Newcastle United	8	4	4	0	11	6	5	16
Liverpool	8	4	2	2	11	9	2	14
Tottenham Hotspur	7	4	1	2	13	12	1	13

Buoyed by their first ever Champions League win (Will had witnessed Kun score an injury time winner to beat Villareal 2-1), City travelled the short distance to Old Trafford for the Manchester derby in late October.

This was the game that would sort the men from the boys. The majority (although a majority that was getting slimmer) expected a United win, which would propel them back above City to the summit.

Nothing could have prepared the authors for what they were about to witness on TV. It was just about the highlight for Will of 37 years following City.

SIX ONE TO CITY!!!! SIX ONE TO CITY!!!!
SIX ONE TO CITY!!!! SIX ONE TO CITY!!!!

Two for Super Mario (he was booked after scoring the first for famously lifting his shirt to reveal a t-shirt proclaiming 'Why Always Me?') , One from Kun, One from Merlin and two late strikes from Edin. The sixth goal had the assist of this and most other seasons as Merlin put Edin through on goal with the kind of pass that mere mortals can only fantasise about!

SIX ONE TO CITY!!!! SIX ONE TO CITY!!!!
SIX ONE TO CITY!!!! SIX ONE TO CITY!!!!

United's biggest home defeat in living memory, Fergie's worst day in football and a MASSIVE statement of intent from City, now with 33 goals in 9 games and 5 points clear.

The texts were pouring in from anybody Will knew who had the remotest interest in football. His wife hugged him like they had just won the lottery. Martyn was speechless, or so it seemed.

In fact, Martyn had not even watched the game, readily accepting the offer to work that afternoon as he needed all the money he could muster for his imminent wedding.

He had suffered too many times in the past watching derby games and now could not even bring himself to watch from behind the sofa. This had crystallised permanently in the late late show at Old Trafford two years previously, when United won 4-3. This match had knocked the stuffing out of Martyn and had taken him days to recover.

He now finds it impossible to enjoy games against United, at least until the final whistle has blown and City have won! In hindsight he probably would have enjoyed this one but had to make do with being happily stunned at receiving Will's text summing up the game. Perhaps next time he will watch!

The jokes soon started, 'a crisis line has been set up for United fans that may be feeling suicidal after the derby result. For help and advice they should call 0161 61 61 61 61!'

City wags mocked the United '19' banners that proclaimed United's 19 League titles, by printing their own '19' banners in sky blue – of course turned upside down they read '61'.

It was the best time ever to be a City fan. Even the media hailed us as potential champions. We had not just beaten them, oh no, this was an anni-hilation. One more time, lest the readers forget...

SIX ONE TO CITY!!!! SIX ONE TO CITY!!!!
SIX ONE TO CITY!!!! SIX ONE TO CITY!!!!

We were suddenly champions elect. United were a spent force. We could be the next 'Invincibles'.

Enough of this hype and euphoria – it's time to get back to the class of '98. The sequence of results after the New Den war zone went D, L, W, L, L. Four points out of a possible 15. Inconsistent City won at fancied Wigan but then promptly lost at lowly Lincoln during this run.

Hardly what we had expected, 11th place with 21 points from 15 games, a meagre 18 goals scored and 16 conceded. Where was our runaway success? Keeping the faith was getting that bit harder.

After the Lincoln defeat, City decided to cut their losses on Lee Bradbury who moved to Palace for exactly half of the £3 million we had paid for him.

Royle decided we needed reinforcing. At last! Were we splashing out the Badbuy cash on a new striker?

Most City fans (authors definitely included) were nonplussed that our would be saviour came in the form of a 28-year-old centre-back, initially signed on loan from Huddersfield by the name of Andy 'Jock' Morrison.

He of dodgy knees and an even dodgier disciplinary record, not to mention an unsavoury reputation away from football as a heavy drinker and trouble maker. Kevin Horlock allegedly remarked to Jock himself, 'we must be desperate if we need you!'

Joe Royle had deemed that we were too nice. We needed a hard man and leader to grab our season by the scruff of the neck before it was too late. Royle believed Jock to be that man, putting him straight in the team.

He promptly scored on his debut, a 2-1 win over Colchester and then inspired City to a 3-0 win at local rivals Oldham, scoring his second goal in two games. As Martyn rightly remembers, the goal at Oldham was a 25-yard screamer of a volley, a goal in a million for a less than agile centre-back.

The loan deal soon became a permanent £85,000 transfer, City moving quickly just in case other suitors emerged having noticed the impact he was having.

Was this the catalyst that Royle had hoped for, the turning point in our season?

Will and old school chum (John) Burfield (a regular contributor to City fanzine King of the Kippax) drove to the next game at Wycombe with renewed hope, even renewed expectation. It was the second week of November and over 8,000 fans packed into tiny Adams Park for Wanderers' Cup Final.

The talk on the drive up was of how Jock would lead us back to the top. We both knew him from our Devon days when he had started his career so promisingly at Plymouth Argyle. He was a natural leader and made of rock.

Wycombe were joint bottom with our last away day conquerors Lincoln. Surely we had learned our lesson not to underestimate minnows in their own pond?

The conversation soon turned into what a stupid location Adams Park was – situated on a trading estate with one road in and the traffic was a nightmare. They couldn't cope with City!

City couldn't cope with Wycombe in fact and the journey home was taken up with depressing conversation, befitting our pathetic 1-0 loss. We certainly didn't give a toss about the traffic! The table made alarming reading:

Team	P	W	D	L	F	A	GS	PTS
Stoke City	18	12	1	5	27	15	27	37
Fulham	16	11	3	2	26	12	26	36
Walsall	18	11	2	5	28	23	28	35
Preston North End	17	9	5	3	32	17	32	32
Gillingham	18	7	8	3	28	18	28	29
Chesterfield	16	8	4	4	17	10	17	28
Manchester City	18	7	6	5	23	18	23	27
Luton Town	16	8	3	5	21	16	21	27

Only seventh again, and worryingly a gap opening up with the leading teams and many others having games in hand. Could it get any worse?

Transporting back to 2011, the resounding United victory really had instilled a feeling of belief in the Sky Blues of Manchester. City won five games on the bounce, scoring 17 goals, including a 3-0 away trouncing of Villarreal in the Champions League. Just as we thought we were cracking it on all fronts, down to earth with a bump!

City travelled to Naples knowing that a draw would probably be enough for us to qualify for the Champions League knockout phase.

The Neapolitan atmosphere was highly charged, with over 50,000 home fans screaming from start to finish. City looked decidedly nervy and it was no surprise when (reported City target) Cavani gave the home side the lead.

15 minutes later, City were level, Mario pouncing on a goalkeeping mistake. All this did though was stoke up the crowd even further and make the home side more determined.

City survived an onslaught, which had Will fidgeting nervously as he watched at home. When Cavani scored again just after half-time, an air of inevitability spread in Naples and Surrey.

Napoli continued to batter us with Hart making several fine saves and Hamsik hitting the post. Their 'keeper made one brilliant save near the end from Mario but Napoli held on for a totally deserved victory.

The City players slumped off dejectedly, knowing that qualification was now out of our hands – we would need to beat Group Winners Bayern at home and hope that Villarreal (nil points from five games) would somehow stop the Italians winning in Spain.

Will just slumped onto the sofa. How expectations had changed, the pain of losing is as bad in the Champions League as it is in lower League football. Sensible perspective would have put a defeat in Naples as way more preferable than a defeat at Lincoln, but since when have football fans been sensible?

City had been hurt badly by that defeat and finished November with an unconvincing 1-1 draw at Anfield in the League (featuring a Mario red card) and by scraping a 1-0 win at the Emirates in the League Cup quarter-final, albeit with a goal of sublime quality from Agüero, set up brilliantly by Džeko and Johnson.

City remained five points clear (and with a goal difference to die for) however, with Spurs emerging as serious title contenders.

Team	P	W	D	L	F	A	GD	PTS
Manchester City	13	11	2	0	43	12	31	35
Manchester United	13	9	3	1	30	13	17	30
Tottenham Hotspur	12	9	1	2	26	16	10	28
Newcastle United	13	7	5	1	19	12	7	26
Chelsea	13	8	1	4	28	17	11	25
Liverpool	13	6	5	2	17	12	5	23
Arsenal	13	7	2	4	26	23	3	23

Around the same period 13 years earlier, City were plumbing new depths to make their fans everywhere despair, even more so as United were doing well domestically and in Europe.

Following the Wycombe debacle, three dismal League draws in which just one goal had been scored, a home defeat to Mansfield in the Football

League Trophy and scraping into the FA Cup third round after beating Mighty Darlington in a replay.

City had splashed the cash again during this period, paying £400,000 for big centre-forward Gareth Taylor, who arrived from Sheffield United. The 25-year-old had a not-too-bad lower League scoring record (41 goals in 154 appearances), and at that low time, us Citizens would take any crumb of comfort.

We had scored a paltry eight goals in 10 games, so clearly we needed more firepower and Gareth would do.

Our last game before Christmas was York City away. This was to be an away day special for Will and Martyn. It had been planned as soon as the fixtures were announced – a nice day out in beautiful York followed by top of the League City demolishing the Minster Men.

Reality was somewhat different of course. If it had been a case of just turning up on the day, we may not even have bothered, especially as Will had a bad bout of man flu. However, with match and train tickets ordered well in advance, uncle and nephew clambered aboard the early train from Kings Cross bound for York.

This was Martyn's Christmas present. Will was thinking that it would be a T-shirt next year, however, Martyn was determined that we would enjoy the day out and did his best to lift his ill and City depressed uncle.

Upon arriving in York at around 10am, he proceeded to cajole his suffering uncle around the city, even making him climb the several hundred steps to the top of York's world famous minster.

The climb had a wonderful effect on Will, clearing his flu symptoms (helped no doubt by countless Beechams flu+) and putting him in a far better frame of mind ('rubbish, Will remained a sniffily grumps for the remainder of the day!' recalls Martyn).

As they strolled over to the tiny Bootham Crescent ground, the talk was of better times ahead, how we could still do it, how a win today would start the table climb, how Gareth Taylor would bang the goals in.

We entered the stadium and were pleased to see the usual strong City contingent among the capacity crowd of just over 7,500.

This was a huge occasion for York, City being the biggest club to visit for a League match in modern times. Just like at Lincoln and Wycombe before, this was their Cup Final. We had lost those games, but there was no way we would lose today!

The ground was real football throwback. The refreshment stand sold wagon wheels and bovril (both eagerly snapped up by Will for a retro fix), there was a brass band playing as pre-match entertainment and the crowd seemed to be virtually on the pitch as they packed onto the tiny terraces and archaic main stand.

There was a definite nervous tension among the City fans that day. There was a feeling that if we did not turn things around and go on a winning streak very soon, we would be condemned to another season at least at this level.

An indication of just how far City had sunk and how alien we were to this League, was that York's tiny away dugout did not have a chance of containing all of our back-room staff, who spilled out almost onto the pitch in all of their shiny Kappa jackets.

As well as Joe and assistant Willie, there was Alex Stepney the goalkeeping coach, Asa Hartford the reserve team manager, the subs and non-playing squad members plus several other fitness coaches, physios, masseurs, conditioning coaches and for all we knew hair stylists and dieticians too!

Contrast this with York's bench that contained their manager, his assistant, the physio and three subs. We were a bloated mess of a club at the time and this summed it up. We would have needed a House of Commons bench to seat our lot!

As the players entered the fray, there seemed to be mainly desperate shouts of 'COME ON, CITY!!' rather than any co-ordinated singing. This clearly wasn't a City atmosphere of excitement and anticipation but one of simply willing City to get the three points.

In contrast, the York fans were there to enjoy the day out. They didn't expect David to slay Goliath but knew that the sleeping giants were vulnerable (especially as Morrison and Dickov were suspended and Goater and Wiekens out with injury and flu respectively). The Sky Blues may have been eight places above York, but only six points separated the two Citys.

The brass band hadn't even had time to pack away their instruments when disaster struck. York took the lead inside the first minute. Will turned to Martyn, 'I don't fu**ing believe it!!' He was 16 now so the no swearing rule no longer applied!

The City faithful were now desperate. We simply cannot lose this one. The desperation permeated onto the pitch, affecting the nervous City players who were treating the ball like the proverbial hot potato.

To be fair, they were giving it a go with York seemingly determined to protect their lead for the next 89 minutes. We pressed and pressed and finally scored an equaliser just after the half hour mark. Boo Boy Craig Russell sent in a cross from the bi-line, which somehow looped over the goalkeeper's head and into the net.

You would have thought City had won the Cup, such was the reaction of the away fans. We had at least been given a day pass out of jail and surely we would now go on to win the game with the momentum absolutely in our favour.

The game continued in pretty much the same vein after the goal. City pressing but York soaking up all we could throw at them. 'Come On City, Come On City,' was the rallying cry from the Blue Brothers (many of whom were situated in the 'home' parts of the ground).

York did not seem to be intent on attacking too much. That was until the 87th minute. They broke forward and we held our breath. The ball was squared across to York's 18-year-old substitute Andrew Dawson who was making his debut and had only been on for one minute.

He calmly slotted the ball past Weaver who had no chance. That was it, game over.

We felt dejected, betrayed, angry and a whole host of other negative emotions. 'You're not fit to wear the shirt!' (a rather snazzy Kappa production as it happened). The fans also turned on the vast bench contingent with chants of, 'you don't know what you're doing, you don't know what you're doing,' aimed at Joe Royle and his assistant Willie Donachie (both former City playing greats – don't they say you should never go back?).

After venting our spleen for another 10 minutes or so we trudged back to the train station. Will's flu had returned with a vengeance and he felt just lousy. Martyn also felt lousy but it had nothing to do with flu.

We were now at our lowest ebb footballing wise. We would be 12th with nearly half the season gone. The first texts arrived, 'in the 12th place at Christmas, my true love gave to me, a misfiring Man City'. 'CITY has been added to the Oxford Book of Acronyms, it stands for Conference In Two Years.' Quite witty for a Leeds fan, Will would have to get him back at some later date if the opportunity ever arose (and boy did it ever!!), he thought and fumed. Phone off!

The table made stark reading for us:

Pos	Team	P	W	D	L	F	A	GS	PTS
1	Fulham	21	14	3	4	33	16	33	45
2	Walsall	22	14	3	5	33	24	33	45
3	Stoke City	22	14	2	6	30	16	30	44
4	Preston N E	21	10	7	4	37	22	37	37
5	Gillingham	22	9	10	3	33	18	33	37
6	Bournemouth	20	9	6	5	32	21	32	33
7	Chesterfield	21	9	6	6	22	15	22	33
8	Millwall	22	8	8	6	22	23	22	32
9	Reading	21	8	7	6	25	27	25	31
10	Wigan Athletic	22	8	6	8	28	22	28	30
11	Luton Town	20	8	6	6	27	23	27	30
12	Manchester City	22	7	9	6	25	21	25	30
13	Blackpool	22	7	8	7	27	27	27	29
14	York City	22	7	6	9	28	37	28	27

On the platform waiting for the York to London, Will noticed a dark suited gentleman deep in thought. It was City (and now FA) chairman David Bernstein who must have thought 'FCUK' at the sight of two City fans – and it had nothing to do with our attire! (Bernstein was also on the board of French Connection UK at the time.)

Will wanted to go up to him to speak, but what could he say? He would be as dejected as the authors were, after all he was a City fan first and foremost just like us.

In the event, they just nodded to each other. We knew exactly how each other was feeling and it didn't need words to convey them.

The train glided in and the hurting Blues went in opposite directions, the authors to their super saver seats, the chairman to his first-class sanctuary. The opportunity had passed.

Will and Martyn shared little conversation on the journey home, preferring their Walkmans and staring out of the window. Football had ruined a grand day out and the immediate future looked bleak.

This was and is standard fare on long trips home. If City win, it goes by in the blink of an eye with conversation flowing. When City lose, invariably the train gets delayed and conversation is minimal. You just want to get home and shut yourself off from football completely. At least until Monday when you start anticipating much better for the next match.

Pre-Christmas 2011 had a whole different outlook of course. Optimism with a capital O. December started with the 5-1 slaughter of Norwich. Will then travelled to the final Champions League Group match v Bayern Munich, a game that saw Martyn make his European debut.

We were confident of victory (Bayern were already through and expected to play a largely second string team) but equally expected to be eliminated (and into the Europa League) with a Napoli win in Spain.

The hairs stood up on Martyn's neck as the CL anthem played – a really special moment when you experience this for the first time.

City comfortably won the match against the German's reserve team (ex-City defender Jerome Boateng was the only first-team regular to play). It finished 2-0 but the anticipated victory for Naples also came through and we were out but not dejected.

The news that United had also been eliminated was met with delight. The seasoned European campaigners had been presented with a seemingly easy group but had been dumped out by unfancied Basle, the Swiss champions.

This meant that they would also have Thursday night football to contend with, the League goalposts were arranged the same way for both clubs.

Next up Chelsea at Stamford Bridge, for Sky's Monday Night Football. A tough looking fixture and so it panned out with City slumping to their first League defeat of the season. It also brought the first controversial incidents of City's season that led us to believe we had been robbed.

City started at a blistering pace and took an early lead through Super Mario after only two minutes. Will punched the air in delight as he watched on telly. Mario was a cult hero to the City masses. Highly unpredictable he may be but there was never a dull moment. Martyn loved him, Will was a little more reticent, but at that moment he was fantastic!

After 15 minutes, a game changing decision. David Silva was blatantly brought down in the box for an absolute stonewall penalty. Yeah, it would be 2-0 to City and already probably game over. But no, unbelievably the referee waved play on.

Will punched the sofa in frustration (don't tell Mrs L!). It was 1-1 at half-time and the game was very much in the balance. Mancini was incensed and made his feelings known to the ref.

Chelsea now had a platform to build on and urged on by their vociferous support, they took the game to City in the second half. Their cause was helped no end with Clichy sent off for two yellow cards inside the first 12 minutes (our third red card in six League games as Mario was dismissed at Liverpool and Kompany had an early bath at home to Wolves).

In the interests of fairness, the referee called that one correctly. It was now backs to the wall time. Agüero was sacrificed for centre-back Kolo Toure and City dug in.

Despite Chelsea peppering the City goal. There seemed no way through. Will was getting very agitated at home and Mrs L. was forced to take the dog for a walk in the dark to escape.

The sofa was punched several times as Chelsea were gifted a winner. A shot was blasted towards goal, striking Lescott on the arm from close range. It was no way arm to ball, to coin a technical phrase, but definitely ball to arm.

Referee Clattenburg pointed to the spot. He had denied us a certain penalty but awarded Chelsea a really dodgy one. Up stepped substitute Lampard, 2-1, game over. Our superb unbeaten run had finally gone after 15 games and City's League lead was down to two points.

City bounced back from this setback with a hard fought home victory against improving Arsenal, 1-0 thanks to Silva's strike, followed by a more comfortable 3-0 against Stoke.

For the first time in 82 years, City were top of the whole pile at Christmas. Yuletide would be an especially happy day for the authors and City fans everywhere. City had delivered a great present unlike the unseasonal package proffered in '98.

Team	P	W	D	L	F	A	GD	PTS
Manchester City	17	14	2	1	53	15	38	44
Manchester United	17	13	3	1	42	14	28	42
Tottenham Hotspur	16	11	2	3	32	19	13	35
Chelsea	17	10	3	4	35	20	15	33
Arsenal	17	10	2	5	33	25	8	32
Liverpool	17	8	6	3	20	13	7	30

The year petered out somewhat with a 0-0 draw at West Brom. We now led on goal difference only. Still the omens were good – whoever was top going into the new year, nearly always won the League.

Whereas 2011 was a festive season of good cheer, contrast that with 1998. In reality we were at our lowest ever League position, 12th in the third tier (although we had been 14th for a while early in the season, this was such early doors to have been relatively insignificant) with half the season gone almost.

We had expected to dominate but that honour seemed to be going Fulham's way, while we were struggling to cope in the way that our detractors had hoped for.

It is to be sincerely hoped that the following words never appear in print again – City faced an absolutely vital game at Wrexham – lose and all could be lost.

For the City wags, this was our European adventure, across the border into Wales. Boxing Day 1998 was the date. Will hadn't enjoyed his turkey and trimmings through worrying about the match.

Martyn and Will were together for Christmas and they left the rest of the family to the traditional cold turkey, mashed potato (coloured purple from beetroot juice of course!) and various pickles, to tune into *Radio Five Live*.

City were one of the featured matches, as they often had been that season despite their lowly status. Even the Beeb seemed to be glorifying in our demise.

The authors remained transfixed to the radio for the entire 90 minutes. First half reports had suggested that Wrexham were the better side, with winger Terry Cooke, on loan from of all teams Manchester United, terrorising the City full-backs, Crooks and Edghill. We managed to get to half-time scoreless. COME ON CITY!!!!

The second half kicked off. Around 10 minutes passed before the scariest words in the footballing world were uttered by the commentator, 'we will be off to the Racecourse Ground in a moment, where there has been a goal'.

Every football fan everywhere will relate to these words. Your heart goes into your mouth, you close your eyes and start praying to a higher Order, you start uttering over and over and over, 'Please! Please! Please! Please!' You start imagining the City fans going wild and the players celebrating, then you start imagining the City fans disconsolate and the players with their heads down.

'Will the United/City/Rovers (or whoever happens to be the commentary match) winger hurry up and take the bloody corner so we can find out what is going on at the only important match being played today!?'

They then bring in Ron Cruickshank, lower League Northern football correspondent. You first hear the crowd – oh my goodness, it sounds quite loud, is that because it is a home goal or maybe because Ron is situated near the City fans?

'And the score here at the Racecourse is… GET ON WITH IT! GET ON WITH IT!… Wrexham nil… YEEEESSSSS!!!! Uncle and nephew never heard the Manchester City one bit, drowned out in the delirium occurring in their parents'/grandparents' Devon home.

They just recovered our composure enough in time to hear the name Wiekens. 'We love you Gerard we do, we love you Gerard we do.' Memories of a Cornish sports quiz came flooding back. Bloody good bloke that Gerard Wiekens.

Despite a few scares, we held on. Was this the start of our run? Could we climb the table at last?

(Martyn laments, 'this sort of magic moment is going to be rarer and rarer now that everyone has got Internet access on their smart phones'. He remembers assuming that City had drawn 0-0 at home to Bradford the previous season when, having switched on BBC1, Manchester City 1 scrolled along the final score vidiprinter. Cue hysterical scenes as Tony Vaughan's headed injury time winner was celebrated wildly. Magic!)

Two days later we came from behind to beat highflying Stoke City 2-1, with Welshman Gareth Taylor scoring an 85th minute winner. Wales had been very kind to us these past few days.

City therefore ended 1998 on a bit of a high, up to seventh and just two points off the Play-off places. Automatic promotion may be beyond us but we had a very clear goal, finish in the top six and win the Play-offs.

Pos	Team	P	W	D	L	F	A	GS	PTS
1	Fulham	23	15	4	4	36	17	36	49
2	Walsall	24	14	4	6	35	28	35	46
3	Stoke City	24	14	2	8	31	19	31	44
4	Preston N E	23	12	7	4	41	23	41	43
5	Bournemouth	22	11	6	5	35	22	35	39
6	Gillingham	23	9	11	3	31	9	31	38
7	Manchester City	24	9	9	6	28	22	28	36
8	Wigan Athletic	24	9	7	8	31	23	31	34
9	Reading	22	9	7	6	26	27	26	34
10	Blackpool	24	8	9	7	29	28	29	33

This is what it meant to be City in '98 – and football is supposed to be a hobby! Good riddance 1998, here's to better times in '99, PLEASE!

Winter Blues

The new 'era' (1999) started with an FA Cup third round match against Premier League Wimbledon.

The game was notable for three things – 1. Will took his future wife Rania to her first ever game (she enjoyed the banter but wondered if it was always that cold at football matches), 2. City played really well against a team two divisions higher up, and 3. Jock Morrison was sent off, meaning he would miss three vital League games due to suspension.

City undeservedly lost 1-0, with all the usual, 'now we can just concentrate on the League', clichés trotted out by fans, players and management alike.

We followed that up with a creditable goalless draw at Blackpool before staring down the barrel of three mammoth looking games – Fulham at home, Walsall away and Stoke away. We were to play the whole top three consecutively, the exact three games for which captain Morrison was suspended.

Joe Royle then negotiated a fine piece of business. Remember Terry Cooke, the United loanee that had run our defence ragged for much of the Boxing Day game? He was now back at United and Royle phoned Fergie to enquire about his availability.

Fergie had always claimed that he wanted City to do well (not 2012 style well, obviously!) and he was more than happy to lend us his reserve of a reserve winger for the rest of the season.

Cooke made his debut in the game against Fulham, who were eight places and 15 points better off than City and stood two points clear at the top of the table with two games in hand on second placed Walsall.

This promised to be a very tough test. That City ran out 3-0 winners was remarkable. We actually played Fulham off the park. Goals from Goater (who was just showing signs of winning over the fans), Taylor and Horlock did the trick. Cooke contributed some nice touches – things were definitely looking up.

Next up on the treble chance, a trip to the Midlands to play the Saddlers at Bescot Stadium. Over 9,500 crammed in for what was in truth more like our Cup Final than theirs.

We left with a very satisfying 1-1 draw, Jamie Pollock equalising in the 74th minute. The authors and our compatriots were starting to believe. Five games unbeaten in the League since the York debacle and only two goals conceded.

Make that two goals conceded in six games. We won perhaps that hardest game of the tricky trilogy, 1-0 at Stoke. Martyn and Will took in the Friday night game separately, Will on Sky TV and Martyn on the radio. City on TV was a rare treat in those days.

Martyn happened to be on a college trip to the theatre that evening but was determined not to miss the action. He listened covertly with one hand over his ear as if he were leaning on it. Subsequently he remembers nothing of the play but was able to respond truthfully to his mum when she asked whether he had had a good time!

We saw/heard Wiekens score an absolute gem of a goal in the 20th minute, a goal worthy of winning any match. Wiekens was superb throughout, marshalling the Jock free defence and making countless interventions and clearing headers. Sheer class, we just hoped the rumours of Premier League scouts watching him were unfounded. He was also our quiz partner after all!

Stoke made us squirm a little but City held out. The large City contingent that had made the short trip were in fine voice, a non-stop rendition of 'Joe Royle's Blue & White Army, Joe Royle's Blue & White Army, Joe Royle's Blue & White Army,' lasting for about 20 minutes.

Will joined in at home but Martyn wisely kept his singing in his head only so as not to bring shame on his college and be found out by his tutors.

We may have finished January in eighth spot, but were now on a roll and only four points off fourth place. It was definitely game on.

Pos	Team	P	W	D	L	F	A	GS	PTS
1	Fulham	27	18	4	5	40	20	40	58
2	Preston	28	16	7	5	51	27	51	55
3	Walsall	28	15	6	7	39	32	39	51
4	Stoke City	27	15	3	9	37	24	37	48
5	Bournemouth	26	13	7	6	43	27	43	46
6	Gillingham	27	11	12	4	42	25	42	45
7	Chesterfield	28	13	6	9	32	23	32	45
8	Manchester City	28	11	11	6	33	23	33	44
9	Millwall	29	11	10	8	34	32	34	43
10	Wigan Athletic	27	11	7	9	38	27	38	40

Ironically, as results started picking up on the pitch for City '99, City 2012 were stuttering a little.

Will endured one of those awful situations on New Year's Day. It was still officially the festive period and he and his wife had been invited to have lunch with some good friends. The only issue was that lunch was arranged for 1pm and with the lady of the house being such a fantastic chef, lunch was always about ten delicious courses.

City were live on TV that very afternoon, kick-off 3pm. Will knew very well that lunch would extend to at least four hours and that is exactly what was happening. Will was in an excrutiating position. Conversation from him had all but dried up as he imagined the position at the Stadium of Light.

Worst still, there was no mobile signal at the friend's house so he could not even surreptitiously get the score on his mobile. Anything could be happening.

Come 4.30pm Will was getting extremely agitated. The friends and Mrs L. noticed that he had been reduced to single word sentences and the odd nod and 'I know'. No I wasn't tired or drunk for goodness sake!

The man of the house, with only a passing interest in football (he supports local club Brighton if pressed), must have realised what was going on, and suggested we take dessert and coffee in the lounge.

Off we trotted and Will stared at the blank TV screen. He was far too polite to ask to watch the game. That would have been frightfully rude. Salvation was at hand from his male friend, however.

'Aren't Manchester City on television today?' he asked. 'Um, I think they might be, I am not 100% sure,' Will completely and utterly lied in response. 'Shall we have a look?' Will's host helpfully suggested. 'Of course we should! Oh, I mean, that would be good if you don't mind.'

Will was more than half expecting this to be followed by the crushing words – 'oh its on Sky Sports is it? I don't have Sky Sports.' But joy of joys, they had Sky Sports.

There were 20 minutes left and the score was 0-0. They showed the possession, shots and corner count and it was clear that City were absolutely hammering Sunderland, but could not score. This was our chance to go three clear as United had inexplicably lost to struggling Blackburn the previous day.

The match continued in this vein for the rest of the game. City were camped in the Black Cats' half. In the 93rd and last minute, Micah Richards smashed a header against the bar and from the rebound they broke clear and into City's penalty box.

The ball was passed to Ji Dong-Won, later proven to be offside, who bundled the ball into an empty net. This was the last kick of the game. City had lost.

Back in Brighton, Will was biting his tongue and sitting on his fist. He wanted to rage but was in polite company, 'blimey, that was bad luck,' quipped the host. Will merely nodded and said 'I know.' (Now time to get drunk and tired!)

A resounding 3-0 victory was secured at home to Liverpool two days later, but at the cost of a sending off for Gareth Barry meaning that he would miss the next match – the little matter of a FA Cup third round tie at home to United.

The build up to the game was the usual intensity. Would it be City asserting their authority to build upon the 6-1 or would it be revenge for United? They had enticed Paul Scholes out of retirement in time to be a substitute on the day, City rested Joe Hart to give Pantilimon a rare start. Barry was of course suspended while Yaya (and brother Kolo) Toure had left for international duty in the African Cup of Nations, where they could be for a month if Ivory Coast as expected got to the Final.

The first half was calamitous, not so much due to City being 3-0 down but more so because Vincent Kompany was unjustly given a straight red for a so called two-footed lunge at Nani. Nani was not hurt in the slightest and certainly did not complain (for once) but Chris Foy deemed it serious foul play and sent Vinny off.

Will did not agree, and let the television know his feelings in the strongest terms possible!

City later appealed but the Premier League had to back their referee so Kompany was banned for four games, as this was his second red of the season. More injustice – this meant that Vinny would be out for both semi-final legs of the League Cup against Liverpool and two League games. He would be missed.

Ten men City clawed it back to 3-2 to restore a lot of pride (Will had feared a 6-1 the other way) but the game and especially the sending off left a really sour taste. With no Vinny and no Kolo, City had to rely on rookie Montenigrin Stefan Savic to fill in.

In the next two games, we lost 1-0 at home to Liverpool in the semi first leg (poor refereeing decision gifting Liverpool a penalty, penalising Savic for a foul that did his confidence no good at all) and scratched out an important 1-0 League win at Wigan thanks to a Džeko header.

Next up in the League were Spurs at the Etihad. This was hyped up as only the media can. Spurs were flying and if they defeated City, they would be only two points behind.

City, shorn of Vinny, Yaya and Kolo (and of course Carlos, still on his self-imposed exile in Argentina), were looking very vulnerable all of a sudden and their mettle was being sorely tested. Was this a sign of City cracking under the pressure?

At half-time it was 0-0, by the 64th minute it was 2-2! Nasri and Lescott put City two up inside the hour, only for Defoe and Bale to get it back all square.

The momentum was now with Spurs. City sent on Balotelli, who was soon involved in a clash with Scott Parker that was to lead to a retrospective sending off and a four game ban.

Lucky for us that the referee hadn't spotted it during the game or we would have been really up against it, a man down for the last 10 minutes.

The game seemed to be heading for a draw, when Gareth Bale sprinted clear in injury time, he squared a tantalising cross across the box for Jermaine Defoe to slide in and knock the ball in for a late winner and put a severe dent into City's title ambitions.

But wait a minute, Defoe failed to connect by centimetres and City were reprieved!

Even better, City then broke clear seconds later, with that man Mario brought down in the box to earn a penalty.

Will (and every other City fan) held his breath. Mario, coolness personified, stepped up to nonchalantly stroke the penalty home for the winner. The ground (and Will's lounge) went wild in celebration.

We had got out of jail. Instead of Spurs breathing down our necks, they were now eight points behind us (and five behind United) to be effectively out of the title reckoning.

Mario's goal also meant we had equalled the number of League goals we scored in the entire previous season with 16 games left!

January was to be a poor month overall however. We went out of the League Cup 3-2 on aggregate, due to another appalling refereeing decision (well dodgy penalty) and a decisive goal from Old Boy Craig Bellamy, and then lost

1-0 at Everton, our old adversaries, with the winner scored by a United loanee!

We thus ended January top only on goal difference, in which was now developing into pretty much a two horse race with our Red neighbours.

Team	P	W	D	L	F	A	GD	PTS
Manchester City	23	17	3	3	60	19	41	54
Manchester United	23	17	3	3	56	21	35	54
Tottenham Hotspur	23	15	4	4	44	25	19	49

February brought five straight wins, with 13 goals scored and only one goal conceded. Three wins came in the League plus victories in both legs of the Europa League tie against holders Porto. Yaya was back (African Nation runner-up) and this seemed to have a galvanising effect. City were now two points clear.

Team	P	W	D	L	F	A	GD	PTS
Manchester City	26	20	3	3	67	19	48	63
Manchester United	26	19	4	3	63	26	37	61
Tottenham Hotspur	26	16	5	5	51	30	21	53

After our January wobble, which had seen the authors start believing in conspiracy theories and even start to question Mancini's managerial ability, the campaign seemed to be back on an even keel. The truth was that we had missed Vinny and Yaya immensely and their return in February was all we had been missing. Or so it seemed…

The 1999 boys could not quite match the 2012 team, but they were to remain unbeaten in February to take their unbeaten League run to 10 games.

Millwall were first brushed aside 3-0, with Terry Cooke scoring his first City goal, an intended cross that flew in at the far post. He also set up Horlock's goal in the match. He'll do we thought.

Then to a quite bizarre game at Bournemouth. This was the authors first 'live' game since York and with our improved form we were hoping for some payback.

Martyn remembers an embarrassing moment prior to the game. He accidentally and very noisily kicked an empty pint glass across a pub car park that was being frequented by loads of City fans. They of course cheered loudly and chanted, 'just how many has he had? Just how many has he had?' Probably just the one but he was only a skinny (and now blushing) 16-year-old.

The game was played on a bog of a pitch and finished in a dour 0-0 draw – nothing unusual about that. Current captain Pollock got himself sent off in the 84th minute – nothing unusual about that. When Kevin Horlock also saw red in the 90th minute for two bookable offences, you could even say there was nothing unusual about that.

That is except for the reason he received the second yellow. Apparently it was for walking aggressively towards the referee! Effectively he was booked for potential dissent, despite the fact that he had not even opened his mouth and did not get within 10 yards of the ref before he brandished the card.

We guessed that this is the first time any player had ever been sent off for what was little more than a Pythonesque silly walk. As a result the Locks (Hor and Pol) would be suspended.

In truth, City were rubbish that day even with 11 men and created nothing at all.

That would be it for a while attendance wise for Will and nephew as Will had just bought a flat in South Croydon and was now as skint as City themselves.

Macclesfield were next up, with the Silkmen despatched 2-0 fairly routinely. Finally, a tricky away game at Chesterfield, who were a tough proposition at their Saltergate ground having won 11 of their 16 matches there. Furthermore, City were weakened due to the suspension of the Locks and Jock.

City came away with a well-won point, courtesy of a Lee Crooks equaliser, a belter from 30 yards out, his first goal for the club.

City ended February in fifth spot and were the division's form team. Blondie were making a chart comeback (UK number one in February 1999 with *Maria*) and City were poised to begin theirs too.

Only leaders Fulham could match City's defensive record – our challenge was being built around the solid base of Weaver, Crooks, Edghill, Morrison and Wiekens. We may not be too pretty to watch, but Royle and Donachie were using their 'dogs of war' prowess to good effect.

Pos	Team	P	W	D	L	F	A	GS	PTS
1	Fulham	30	20	5	5	46	23	46	65
2	Preston N E	32	18	8	6	61	32	61	62
3	Walsall	32	18	7	7	44	34	44	61
4	Gillingham	31	14	14	3	44	27	48	55
5	Manchester City	31	13	12	6	38	23	38	51
6	Bournemouth	29	14	8	7	48	29	48	50
7	Stoke City	29	15	3	11	37	30	37	48
8	Wigan Athletic	30	13	7	10	44	30	44	46

Understandably we entered March full of confidence. So what do we go and do next? Draw 0-0 at home to struggling Northampton, that's what! Will had given up expecting anything from City. It was best just to wait and see. They were certainly known as coupon busters in Will's local bookmakers.

Defensively we were great but 38 goals in 32 games at this level was just not good enough. Only Goater had double figures with 10. Bearing in mind the cash shelled out for Dickov, Russell (swapped for Nicky Summerbee but supposedly valued at £1 million) and Taylor, this was a paltry return, especially bearing in mind the creativity of Horlock, Bishop and latterly Cooke.

Goals scored could also be vital as this was the differentiator if teams were level this season, rather than goal difference.

Next up were Burnley away for a midweek fixture that was expected to be a blood and thunder but tight North West derby. 16 Burnley home games had only yielded 32 goals, while 16 City away games had garnered even fewer with 29.

Burnley had however conceded five in their previous home game, so you never know. The result? 6-0 to City! Now every City fan believed. Shaun Goater grabbed a hat-trick in five second half minutes. 'Feed the Goat and he will score,' was starting to gain momentum for what was to become a legendary City song.

City were now sixth (right on the Play-off qualification mark) and had a five point buffer over seventh placed Stoke. With an easy looking home game with Oldham to come, life was beginning to take a rosy hue.

The rosy hue soon wilted and faded away as City crashed against local rivals Oldham. The expression, 'after the Lord Mayor's show', could have been tailor-made for City. Time and time again over the years the fans have had their expectations lifted only for a short sharp reality check to swiftly follow.

City lost 2-1 and the doubters cleared their throats once more to decry City's chances. City didn't exactly dispel their doubts in the next game, a workmanlike 2-1 win at home to struggling Notts County.

This was still a tough time to be supporting City. The best that we could hope for was qualifying for the Play-offs and they were notoriously a lottery. Rarely did they go to form/favourites status and with the Final due to be at Wembley, the Lord Mayor himself would probably be there in person to give City a two-fingered salute!

Will and Martyn spoke on the phone a lot. We surely had the quality in attack with the Goat, Dicky and Cooke, the midfield had enough creativity about it through Super Kev and Bish, while the defence, expertly organised by Morrison (by now captain in place of Pollock) and flourishing 'keeper Weaver, were a match for anybody.

So why couldn't we feel confident? We refer you to the Lord Mayor.

After a very important away win at Colchester, 1-0 thanks to the Goat (and the first ever pay per view game in English football history – £7.95 for the privilege but probably not a great money spinner!) it was time for Martyn and Will to make a long awaited comeback at Reading.

Will had his parents staying in his new flat and having double booked, he managed to talk them into joining him and their eldest grandson at the match. So Reading's record crowd at their Madejski Stadium was to be swelled by two pensioners whose only interest in City was a paternal one.

There was a hugely impressive City contingent that day; there must have been 4,000 Sky Blues. Reading, who had been relegated with City the previous season, were one place and five points behind us, so this was a Play-off six pointer.

Reading were also in fine form, having won four of their previous five games including a 4-0 victory at Stoke. This was a big game, hence over 20,000 came to witness it, the larger than expected crowd leading to a 30 minute delay to kick-off.

We were tense, even Will's mother, more accustomed to biting her nails at Somerset cricket matches, looked nervous.

Finally we were up and running. The atmosphere was superb and City came flying out of the traps. In possibly our best performance of the season, City won through 3-1 with two superb free-kick goals from Terry Cooke and one from the Goat.

Ever the perfectionist, Will chastised City for conceding a last minute consolation (Weaver was closing in on the MCFC clean sheet record), but of course if you had offered us a 3-1 victory at the outset, we would have snapped your hand off.

Mother/Grandmother confessed her affection for Paul Dickov. The City live wire had given an all action display and had really impressed her. Dicky was now officially her favourite current player, joining the ranks of Lawrie McMenemy, Bobby Moore and Trevor Brooking in her footballing faves list.

As we waited for the bus to take us back to Reading Station, we were cheered to hear of a hat-trick from United's Paul Scholes. Strange you may think, only this was for England (now under the temporary management of Fulham's Kevin Keegan) in a 3-1 Euro 2000 qualifier against Poland at Wembley. Oh happy day!

So City finished March in a very healthy fifth place, vitally seven points clear of seventh placed Wigan and in pole position to make the Play-offs coming down the home straight. We were in turn now only seven points behind second placed Preston. We couldn't pinch automatic promotion could we?

Pos	Team	P	W	D	L	F	A	GS	PTS
1	Fulham	37	26	6	5	63	26	63	84
2	Preston N E	37	21	9	7	68	35	68	72
3	Walsall	36	20	8	8	51	40	51	68
4	Bournemouth	37	19	10	8	58	34	58	67
5	Manchester City	38	17	14	7	52	28	52	65
6	Gillingham	37	16	14	7	59	34	59	62
7	Wigan Athletic	35	17	7	11	55	35	55	58
8	Reading	38	15	12	11	48	49	48	57

Reflecting back, this was the day that we knew (as best you can with City!) that we would have a good chance of promotion, almost certainly via the Play-offs.

There was an air of confidence about City, the Goat was scoring, Cooke was firing on all cylinders, Jock was immense and Weaver looked pretty impregnable. The authors allowed themselves to be confident, not cock-sure, just confident.

In 2012 confidence was about to drain away. March is always the time of mad hares and this year there would be some pretty mad City fans too. With all the weaponry at City's disposal, we were well and truly aiming at our own feet.

The month started OK with an easy 2-0 at home to relegation threatened Bolton thanks to Clichy's first City goal (wicked deflection to wrong foot their 'keeper) and Mario.

By the end of that weekend, the gap between United and us remained two points. Worryingly, United had come through a difficult looking run of fixtures largely unscathed.

They had come from three down at Chelsea to draw 3-3, beat fiercest adversaries Liverpool, scored a fortuitous victory at Norwich with a last minute Giggs goal and had comfortably won their biggest banana skin game, 3-1 at Spurs.

We just could not shake them off our tails. They were not playing particularly well but the right results (for them) kept coming. They were notorious at doing this during the run in and it usually grinds fellow challengers down. Think 'I'd love it' Kevin Keegan and you will get what I mean.

Fergie calls it, 'squeaky bum time' and attempts to wind up his opponents by getting at the managers in his mind games – he is pretty good at it and as well as Keegan he has managed to get the likes of Wenger, Benitez and Mourinho to lose their rag in the past. Would Mancini fall into the same trap?

Mancini was to get pretty irate as it happened but this was not directed Fergie's way, it was the players who were experiencing his ire.

A sloppy 1-0 defeat in Lisbon against Sporting in the Europa League was followed by another single goal defeat at Swansea. CITY WERE NO LONGER TOP! Having led the way since early October, we had surrendered the lead at just the wrong time, now being a point behind.

The pundits had a field day. THEY were now favourites. Past masters, they had seen it all before, nearly all their remaining fixtures looked winnable while City had a much harder run in, City didn't have the mental strength etc., etc.

The authors and probably most City fans bought this although there was still one saving grace. United had to visit City with three games to go – it was still in our hands.

One week later we faced Chelsea at home in what all and sundry proclaimed as a must win game if City were to have a chance of staying with their neighbours.

City had bowed out of Europe on the Thursday. The game however was to re-ignite the City winning mentality that had waned somewhat in recent weeks. 2-0 down at half-time (3-0 on aggregate) we were facing humiliation and worse still a confidence sapping defeat.

The second half though was just like the United cup tie in January with one-way City traffic towards the Sporting goal. With only 30 minutes to go, the score remained the same. With nine minutes to go, the aggregate scores were level after two goals from Kun and a Mario penalty. Game on!

In the last minute of injury time, City won a corner. Joe Hart quietly trotted into the Lisbon penalty area. The corner came over and Hart met it with a goal bound header only for their 'keeper to deny his opposite number with a fantastic save to tip the ball around the post.

City had lost but had won in many ways – they showed they had resolve, would never give up and perhaps most importantly they restored the faith of the fans.

Will and Martyn texted each other many times that evening with the theme being that City were up for the fight, there would be no meek surrender. We just wished that David Silva could find the mesmerising pre-Christmas form, then we would surely be OK.

To add more good news, the prodigal had returned. Tevez was back. He had 'apologised' to City for his absence, he had accepted the club fine and wanted to put it all behind him to fire City to the Premier League Title.

After three weeks of intensive training, Tevez was nearing match fitness after all those months of playing golf and appearing on chat shows in his native Argentina. He was fit enough to be named on the bench for the Chelsea game.

City kicked off four points behind United who had thumped Wolves at Molineux 5-0 a few days earlier. Ours was a Wednesday night game to accommodate Chelsea's previous weekend FA Cup quarter-final. The pressure was well and truly on.

Chelsea were resurgent since sacking Villas-Boas and appointing another Roberto, Italian former Chelsea player Di Matteo. They had won six on the bounce and had even progressed to the Champions League semis by overturning a 3-1 first leg deficit against City's CL nemesis, Napoli. They therefore came into the game high on confidence.

After an hour, City fell behind for the first time at home in the League that season. Will stared at the television in disbelief, a feeling of despair gripping him. After dominating the match, it was unbelievable that we were losing. We were throwing the title away, fate it seemed was seeing to that!

Martyn texted, 'time for Tevez, keep the faith', Five minutes later he joined the fray to a largely positive crowd reaction. 'Come on Carlos,' Will shouted encouragingly at the screen. Fickle like most fans, Will had been of the opinion that he should never set foot in Manchester again only a few weeks before. But now we needed him!

With less than quarter of an hour to go we were still losing. On the basis that even a draw wasn't good enough, City were indeed blowing it, the chances seemingly drying up.

Then in the 77th minute, a stroke of fortune. Essien inexplicably handled a Nasri shot inside the area. PENALTY!!

Up stepped Agüero (usual penalty taker Mario had been substituted at half-time) to coolly slot home. We were back in the game, but needed to find a winner from somewhere. Buoyed by the equaliser, City laid siege to the Chelsea goal.

Then, with only four minutes of normal time remaining, Samir Nasri played a neat 1-2 with that man Tevez before deftly easing the ball past the on-rushing Petr Cech to give us the oh so vital three points. City had now won 20 consecutive home games in the League, a Premier League record.

We had done it, out of jail again. Excellent Sky TV pundit (and recently retired ex-United hate figure) Gary Neville called it a title-winning come-back from the dead. As time would tell, that was nothing!

Do you remember what I said about the Lord Mayor? Well, he was to leave his calling card again for the next two matches, while Old Trafford was the destination of choice for Lady Luck.

The fixture list threw up a tough looking Saturday teatime game at Stoke, never an easy place to visit. Stoke have a narrow pitch, designed to suit them and allow them to bomb long throws and crosses into the opponent's area. They are also well known for tough (but fair) tackling and a never-say-die attitude. City did not have a great record there, and without injured trio Kun, Vinny and Lescott, this was to continue. The game was televised once more and the cameras captured a once in a lifetime strike from City's old adversary, Peter Crouch, giving Stoke the lead after an hour. Was he to have a massive influence on City for a third season running?

There seemed to be little danger when the ball was headed to him wide of the right-hand side of the pitch. There were plenty of covering defenders and his position so far from goal could hardly be described as dangerous.

The sofa occupying Will was in a state of disbelief once more as Crouch teed the ball up before crashing a superb dipping volley from 25 yards out that flew over Joe Hart to find the top left-hand corner of the net. NO WAY!

Again a draw was not really good enough, so when Yaya equalised after 76 minutes (his shot being helped home by the Stoke 'keeper), most City fans including the authors, expected another late winner.

It did not transpire unfortunately. Now City were level on points with United but they had a game in hand. We still had a better goal difference and that potentially defining home derby to come so the post match texting analysis still made the title race in City's hands. That could have been a vital point.

United were at home to Fulham on the Monday night. They won 1-0 with Fulham having a blatant penalty turned down in the last minute. They escaped with the win so now stood three points clear. Referees were definitely a sore topic with City at the moment.

We entertained Sunderland the following Saturday, with United not due to play again until the Monday at Blackburn.

Consecutive home victory 21 would surely be ours, to put the pressure back on United for their trip to Ewood Park.

With five minutes to go at the Etihad we were 3-1 down. Even Bendtner had scored for goodness sake! Our home form, the foundation from which we had built everything, was about to let us down when we least needed it to.

Mancini was going berserk on the touchline, completely baffled by our form that afternoon.

That late Mario and Kolarov goals stole us a point hardly seemed to matter. We were blowing it. A point was virtually useless.

United eased to victory at Blackburn. Going into our April fixtures we were now five points behind United and our once double-digit goal difference advantage was down to just one goal. We had a huge mountain to climb and now were relying on others' results against United.

Team	P	W	D	L	F	A	GD	PTS
Manchester United	31	24	4	3	76	27	49	76
Manchester City	31	22	5	4	75	25	50	71
Arsenal	31	18	4	9	62	41	21	58

Will was on a big downer. Even if City beat United, we still needed them to lose another, even if we won all of our games. Highly unlikely he thought.

Where had it gone wrong? Bad refereeing hadn't helped but then again they do say things even themselves out – for every incorrect sending off (Vinny) there is one we got away with (Mario, at first anyway), for every debatable penalty conceded (x two v Liverpool) there is another one given (AJ's v Wolves) etc. No, we were losing it fair and square and seemed to be on the slippery slope to runners-up spot.

Spring Into Action

What a fantastic time of year. Spring is in the air, daffodils are in full bloom and it is the business end of the football season. You have the Easter holiday weekend, usually featuring two games in a few days, to look forward to and if you are really lucky you finally get to sit outside.

In most seasons, the business end for City is either mid-table obscurity or a relegation/promotion fight. Since the sheikhs arrived in town things were different. There was European qualification to be earned, cups to be won and in this eventful 2011-12 season, the biggest one of all was possible – the Premier League title.

But City seemed to be plucking defeat from the jaws of victory. Having led the table for months, we seemed to be cracking under the pressure of 'squeaky bum time'. Will's United acquaintances (so hard to call them mates) certainly thought so judging by the cocky texts he was receiving. It was normal service for them, they had been there, seen that and bought the tacky T-shirt.

Will decided to get away from it all for Easter and booked a cottage in the middle of nowhere (Pembrokeshire) – there was no Sky TV, no working radio and you only got a mobile phone signal stood in the bathtub and only then if the phone was touching the hot tap.

If the title was lost as he suspected, he didn't want to see Gary Neville, he didn't want to hear Alan Green and he certainly did not want all those texts from United (and Leeds, and Pompey, and Everton, and Liverpool, and Ipswich) fans.

The Easter Sunday fixtures had United at home to QPR (worst away record in the League) at lunchtime, followed by City travelling to third placed Arsenal. United winning was a foregone conclusion. This meant City would start at the Emirates a whopping eight points behind with five games to play. Never in the history of the Premier League had any team ever clawed that back.

Mancini conceded that if that actually did happen, it would be impossible for City to win the title.

The Orange/hot tap communication link decided it would not function on Sunday. Mrs L. had cooked a wonderful lamb dinner. Will suggested they take the dog for a walk to help digestion of the delicious meal. He was really hoping to pick up a signal somewhere.

A couple of fields away, he got a signal. Beep, beep, beep. Texts confirmed that United had won 2-0. QPR had had a player unjustly sent off and conceded a ridiculous penalty courtesy of Ashley Young's dive. City was 0-0 after 30 minutes. Will asked Martyn to keep him posted.

From that moment on, the wildflowers, the spring lambs, the sun shining through the trees, were all just window dressing. Will's mind was elsewhere. He had come to Wales to get away from it all and now he was right back in it. City may be eight points behind. United's goal difference is one better than ours. They have now scored more goals than us. Arsenal are fighting Spurs, Newcastle and Chelsea for two Champions League places.

He checked the mobile every five minutes. Signal fine but no texts, must still be 0-0. A point at the Emirates is a good result. Seven points behind with five to play, it can be done. We could nick it like we did in the League

Cup quarter-final – come on Kun! Five points behind with five to play and United still to come to City, that was doable. A win at Arsenal would send a huge signal of intent to United and boost our confidence. It must be nearly time by now, come on City!

Will was completely lost in thought when he was brought back to consciousness by the beep coming from his pocket. He checked his watch; the game must have finished surely.

He gingerly reached for his mobile. Message received! One word told the story. Arteta. No swear words, no details, just Arteta. We had lost, we were eight points behind, we had conceded the title. Phone was switched off rapidly.

A strange feeling came over Will. Not anger, not despair but relief. Relief it was all over, relief that he could stop hoping for the impossible, relief that he could now relax and enjoy the honour of being runner-up.

Martyn felt exactly the same, happy that we were now completely out of it. It's the hope that's the killer. Now we had no hope Martyn felt liberated.

The rest of the walk was very pleasant. Will was 'back in the room' and amazingly in a good mood. When he got back, he got drunk and went to bed without watching *Match of the Day*.

On the Wednesday were the next round of matches. Will studied the remaining fixtures – United were at improving Wigan tonight, while City were at home to safely mid-table West Brom. He texted Martyn, 'I fancy Wigan to get something tonight, if they get a draw and we win all of our games (including United at home), we only need them to lose one of the other three fixtures and Everton at home and Sunderland away are not easy games'.

Winning all our games meant not only beating United, but also winning at Newcastle, whose home form was awesome and who were chasing Champions League qualification. A tall order, notwithstanding the points United needed to drop.

That evening, Rania and Will went to the local pub for dinner. Will put the big matches to the back of his mind as best he could, although he was pleased to see that he had a mobile phone signal.

Martyn came up trumps, Agüero putting City ahead after five minutes. We were doing our bit, now we just need Wigan to get a point. Wigan were actually the form team of the League at the time, belying their status in the relegation zone. They had won four of their last five games, including blitzing Newcastle 4-0 and also winning at the Emirates.

Half-time City led 1-0 (Martyn texted that it should have been two or three more), while the Wigan game was goalless. Five minutes into the second half, the phone beeped. Wigan were only leading 1-0! Fifteen minutes later we were four up. Kun again, Carlos with his homecoming goal and Merlin Silva.

We had better stay for another drink. Will would like to apologise to his wife now for the fact that he did not hear anything she said for the next half an hour. Then came the text that he was waiting for. United had lost. The deficit was down to five again and we restored our goal difference advantage to plus three. Mancini still said we could not do it.

When Will got back, he got drunk and went to bed after watching *Match of the Day*.

This was the state of play when we left the 1998/99 season:

Pos	Team	P	W	D	L	F	A	GS	PTS
1	Fulham	37	26	6	5	63	26	63	84
2	Preston N E	37	21	9	7	68	35	68	72
3	Walsall	36	20	8	8	51	40	51	68
4	Bournemouth	37	19	10	8	58	34	58	67
5	Manchester City	38	17	14	7	52	28	52	65
6	Gillingham	37	16	14	7	59	34	59	62
7	Wigan Athletic	35	17	7	11	55	35	55	58
8	Reading	38	15	12	11	48	49	48	57

City had eight to play, fewer games than all the teams above and immediately below them. Still, we were the form team, no reason that we couldn't win all eight and really go for second place. Let's think BIG! Easter weekend threw up two intriguing North West derbies, both of huge relevance to the promotion picture. First up Wigan (the United conquerors of April 2012) at home and the chance to put City 10 points clear of them (or for Wigan to get within two points of City with three games in hand!), followed by Preston away on Easter Monday and the chance to close the gap on them to four points (or for Preston to put second beyond City).

Things were looking up even before we kicked off against Wigan. Both Preston and Bournemouth lost on the Friday night. Things were looking even better – two wins and we would only be a point behind second placed Preston!

A bumper crowd of over 31,000 swept into Maine Road to enjoy the football in the sunshine. One more reason to love April. One of life's great pleasures is to see your team play on a sunny day wearing your sleeveless replica shirt, shorts and sunglasses. Perhaps those Rugby Leaguers have got it right. Then again, perhaps the joy is in the novelty, a bit like a City home goal under Stuart Pearce.

The game was as tight as expected. Will listened on the radio – it was a featured game on *BBC Radio Sport*, that's how he knew that it was sunny and tight.

A single goal took the points, happily it was for Terry Cooke and City. Not quite the radio drama of the Wrexham Boxing Day game, but butterflies all the same as the immortal, 'there has been a goal at Maine Road', was broadcast.

City were up to fourth and travelled to Preston's Deepdale smelling blood. We had played more games than anybody, but keep winning and anything is possible. That is what Will told Martyn and he had said it so much that he was really starting to believe it.

That was until Preston scored in the first minute. He hadn't even turned on the radio at that time so when he heard, 'goal at Preston', after 20-odd minutes, he assumed it was to break the deadlock. After he heard 'Preston 1', he was mightily relieved to hear it followed by 'Manchester City 1'.

Swearbox Browner had scored a rare goal, albeit a streaky deflection but Will didn't care and neither did the 5,000+ City fans that the radio match analyser estimated were going wild at that precise moment.

That was the end of the scoring with the rest of the game most notable for the customary bookings for Morrison and Pollock and a substitute appearance for on loan former United starlet Mark 'Bobbins' Robins of 'saving Fergie's bacon with a winner in the Cup at Forest' fame.

Suffice to say he didn't have the same effect at City, appearing just twice in total, without troubling the scorers.

So we had missed the chance to go second and in all probability had missed out on automatic promotion.

The following Saturday we played Lincoln at home. Due to the lowly opposition with tiny support and the fact that automatic promotion was almost certainly now beyond us, the crowd dropped by nearly 5,000 from the Wigan game.

City strolled the game 4-0 with Dickov getting his first City hat-trick, in a 14 minute spell either side of half-time.

With other results going our way, we were back up to fourth and only two points behind second. Will told Martyn that anything was possible. Martyn no longer believed his uncle, pointing out that we only had five games left. It's good to be an optimist!

Pos	Team	P	W	D	L	F	A	GS	PTS
1	Fulham	39	28	6	5	66	26	66	90
2	Walsall	39	22	8	9	54	41	54	74
3	Preston N E	40	21	10	9	71	40	71	73
4	Manchester City	41	19	15	7	58	29	58	72
5	Gillingham	40	19	14	7	65	36	65	71
6	Bournemouth	40	20	10	10	61	38	61	70
7	Wigan Athletic	38	18	7	13	57	38	57	61

A top six finish and the Play-offs did, however, look extremely likely, barring a vindictive series of appearances by the Lord Mayor. Fulham looked to be closing in on a century of points.

Luton were brushed aside at HQ four days later. 2-0 after 10 minutes (Dickov again and a very rare Vaughan effort) and 2-0 it stayed.

City won 2-0 again a few days later at promotion rivals Gillingham. This really was their Cup Final and over 10,000 fans crammed into the tiny stadium, hoping to see the Pride of Kent dent the Pride of Manchester. City won fairly comfortably and were now third, four points above fourth placed Preston and only two behind Walsall. OK so they had two games in hand and we had only three to play, but anything IS possible, isn't it?

Pos	Team	P	W	D	L	F	A	GS	PTS
1	Fulham	41	29	6	6	69	27	69	93
2	Walsall	41	24	8	9	57	41	57	80
3	Manchester City	43	21	15	7	62	29	62	78
4	Preston N E	42	21	11	10	74	44	74	74
5	Gillingham	42	19	14	9	65	41	65	71
6	Bournemouth	42	20	11	11	61	39	61	71
7	Stoke City	41	19	6	16	54	53	54	63
8	Wigan Athletic	39	18	8	13	59	40	59	62

So City went into the home game against third bottom Wycombe full of confidence and Will hoping for revenge for that awful November defeat and traffic jam.

Walsall had used up one of their games in hand with a defeat at Preston in the midweek and faced an away trip to Lincoln who were fighting for their lives. City fans and team alike smelt a real chance, especially as Walsall still had to play certain champions Fulham.

If City won and Walsall did not, we would be second on goals scored. Some incentive!

After all the ups and downs and the cause that at times looked hopeless, there was now genuine optimism that we could pinch second spot and automatic promotion.

As mentioned before in this book, City are the proverbial football coupon busters, you should expect the unexpected and that is exactly what happened.

City lost, Walsall won. Chance of second gone and suddenly we were again fretting about whether we would even make the Play-offs with seventh placed Wigan having four games in hand that could put them within touching distance of us.

Time travel to 14 April 2012; destination Norwich. City had their mojo back. With that 4-0 walloping of the Baggies, City had got their scoring touch back after something of a barren run.

City had in fact suffered a miserable goalscoring run away from home with a measly five goals in their last 10 away League games, a run that had brought just nine points.

Compare that with 23 goals in their first six away games with 16 points accrued in that run and you will soon see why City had surrendered the League leadership.

To have the remotest chance of winning the League, City would need to build on the West Brom win and start to find the net on a regular basis again.

Will had secured a ticket for the visit to the Canaries, a 12.45 kick-off. He met up with the rest of the London Supporters' Club travelling party at Liverpool Street Station. There was a relaxed and jovial mood among the City fans that early morning.

Nobody expected us to renew our challenge and with the pressure off, we were here to enjoy the day out.

Carrow Road was a lucky ground for Will – well he had been there twice and we had won twice. The first time was the first game of the 82-83 season, which just so happened to coincide with Will being on a Cambridgeshire fruit picking holiday with two of his Devonian mates.

City won 2-1 with Paul Power scoring first and David Cross getting the winner. The second win was in the early '90s when he went up with the South West Supporters' Club and Adrian Heath scored the only goal.

Will was therefore a good luck charm for the day. It would be nice to keep up the 100% record he thought.

It was a lovely sunny day (sunglasses but no shorts) and after a couple of pints Will joined the healthy turn out of Blues in the ground. Carrow Road had changed a fair bit since Will's last visit and was now a nice modern venue.

Martyn, Maine Road mid '90s.

City players thank the fans before QPR '98 and then make us suffer!

Will's £1 ginger 'loan' cheque for those blinkin' City tickets.

Will and Wife share an expensive beer in Copenhagen.

Get in the net, you beauty! An enthusiastic fan oscillates wildly in the safety net after a City goal in Copenhagen.

Left: Roberto Mancini on the victory bus celebrating City's FA Cup win.

Below: Mancini & daughter, end of season lap of honour in 2011 after securing Champions League qualification.

Vinny leads the Poznan, after the semi-final win against United at Wembley.

Cup Final day in Surrey.

Will holds the Cup.

In need of an updated mirror (and United can shove their '35 Years' banner up…)

Maine Road with its 'odd' stands in 2002.

Main entrance at Maine Road with its metallic cladding.

City of Manchester Stadium – now known as the Etihad.

City mascot Moonchester listens intently to the band at
Bootham Crescent.

Premiership rugby match between Exeter & Northampton – Will was watching
but his mind was elsewhere.

Supporters' flags at the final ever game at Maine Road in 2003.

Will on the pitch with Dunney and friends prior to home game against Newcastle in 2007.

This city is ours! City fans take over a central Copenhagen pub.

Martyn's Grand Day Out – Welcome to York City.

The Irish pub next to Moulin Rouge where Will enjoyed the vital Newcastle game.

City Chippy's rival Blue Moon Chippy opposite the Maine Road stadium.

Just before the start of the penultimate game at Maine Road against West Ham in 2003.

Above: Pre-match at the Wembley semi-final – United fans had yet to arrive.

Below: Post-match at the Wembley semi-final – United fans long since gone!

Will as a baby with his older siblings – already in City colours, a coincidence or pre-ordained?

Younger nephew Josh pictured with Micah Richards in 2006.

Uncle and brother recruited Josh to the cause before he knew how to choose for himself!

Martyn finished the London Marathon and immediately turned his thoughts to City.

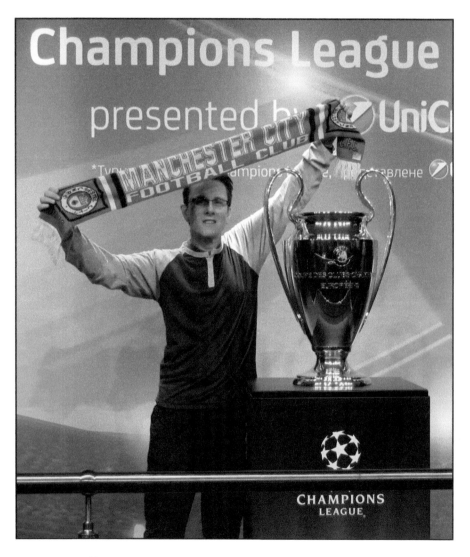

Will gets close to the 'Big One' during a visit to Kiev in 2011.

Will stood (redundant seat once more) and joined in the banter with the home fans, 'top of the League and you fu**ed it up', they taunted us, 'we'll fight 'til the end,' was our instant tuneful reposte.

Once we kicked off you could tell that City were in the mood, stroking the ball around with aplomb and looking dangerous on every attack. Norwich also looked bright and a good game seemed to be brewing up.

Both sides were intent on going forward and having a right go, however, there appeared to be no danger whatsoever when Tevez cut in from the right and smashed the ball home from a tight angle.

That was in the 18th minute and fewer than 10 minutes later, his Argentine strike partner made it two after a great interchange between the club and country teammates.

The City hordes broke swiftly into song (to the tune of *This is how it feels to be Lonely* by the Inspiral Carpets), 'This is how it feels to be City, this is how it feels to be small, you signed Phil Jones, we signed Kun Agüero, Kun Agüero, Kun Agüero'. (Phil Jones was United's big money summer signing, the inference being that we had done the best close-season business of the rival clubs.)

2-0 at half-time and City were cruising. Win number three in Norfolk seemed a formality for Will. Norwich promptly pulled one back five minutes into the second half and for the following 10 minutes or so, City were under the cosh.

Mancini then replaced £25 million Samir Nasri with £24 million Yaya Toure and City soon went on overdrive. Tevez got two more to complete his hat-trick, Agüero scored again and Adam Johnson completed the rout.

City had won 6-1 away for the second time that season and in doing so sent a real message of intent to United. We had just scored more goals in that game than in our previous 10 away League matches! The City fans stayed for several minutes to applaud their heroes. The belief was definitely returning on both sides of the advertising hoardings.

We seemed to be back to our free-scoring days that we had seen at the start of the season. Ten goals in two games and gap down to two points, over to you United. They beat Villa 4-0 next day (another penalty from an Ashley Young dive to set them on the way), to leave the table looking like this:

Team	P	W	D	L	F	A	GD	PTS
Manchester United	34	26	4	4	82	28	54	82
Manchester City	34	24	5	5	85	27	58	77
Arsenal	33	20	4	9	66	41	25	64

Four games to go and a five-point gap. On paper United were still red-hot favourites, but still had to come to our place. If only they would drop a couple of points in one of their other three fixtures, we would win the title if we won all of our games.

The following Sunday, Sky TV had one of their 'Super Sundays', United at home to Everton up first and then City at Wolves.

Will had chosen the occasion to attend his third ever Rugby Premiership match, Exeter Chiefs v Northampton Saints. He tried his hardest to take in the action played for the most part in driving rain but could not help his mind wandering a few hundred miles northwards, where a different shaped ball was in play.

Text number one from Martyn, 30 odd minutes into the Old Trafford match, 'Everton are winning!!!!' The rugby fans around him thought it strange when Will punched the air during a break in play at the rugby. Almost instantly it seemed, text number two arrived, 'bastard, Rooney'. Will punched his seat unnoticed.

An age went by (about 45 minutes in fact) before text number three arrived, 'I thought Everton would put up a better fight defensively than that'. What does he mean? No text for ages must have meant it had stayed 1-1 for ages, surely? A swift text exchange confirmed that United were in fact 4-2 up. It should have been 5-2 with Evra heading against the inside of the post from point blank range.

Well thank you buster! Not exactly Mr Reliable! Will was actually being a tad unfair on his nephew who had faced the small matter of running the London Marathon that day and was now in Covent Garden with his soon to be wife. Then the phone rang, it was Martyn. What does this mean now?

'Will, you won't believe this, it's 4-4 and they are in injury time. Everton have got two goals in seven minutes. United are attacking, oh no, brilliant save by Howard! It's all over. It's in our hands now!' At the end of the rugby match, Will couldn't get to his car quick enough. He wanted to hear the first half on the radio from Molineux before getting to his parents' home in time to watch the second half. Surely we wouldn't blow this opportunity against lowly Wolves!

They were to make heavy weather of it, forcing a frustrated Will to swear several times in front of his Dad and wife before Kun relieved the tension with a well taken goal.

Will saw Nasri's second half clincher. City were now just three points behind United and with a goal difference advantage of six. If we beat United next week we will be top! Mancini still claimed that United were favourites. Will prayed he was wrong.

May The Force Be With Us

Back to 1999 and Will was deflated after another Wycombe debacle, this time at home on the last Saturday in April. A week later a 2-2 draw at Bristol Rovers coupled with another Walsall win mathematically ended any slight chance of City finishing second and going up by right. The point gained did, however, guarantee City's Play-off spot. A lottery maybe, but at least City had a ticket.

City walloped York 4-0 in the last game to clinch fourth spot and secure a two legged Play-off semi-final against Wigan (who had edged out Bournemouth on goals scored). That'll teach the Ministermen to ruin the author's Christmas Day!

Young midfielder Jeff Whitley scored his first City goal in that game (having got two already in the season while on loan at Wrexham).

The other semi would see Gillingham playing Preston for a place in the Wembley Final.

Final League Table

Pos	Team	P	W	D	L	F	A	GS	PTS
1	Fulham	46	31	8	7	79	32	79	101
2	Walsall	46	26	9	11	63	47	63	87
3	Manchester City	46	22	16	8	69	33	69	82
4	Gillingham	46	22	14	10	75	44	75	80
5	Preston N	46	22	13	11	78	50	78	79
6	Wigan Athletic	46	22	10	14	75	48	75	76
7	Bournemouth	46	21	13	12	63	41	63	76

Footnote: Fulham did get over 100 points but Keegan promptly resigned to take over England full-time.

City travelled to Wigan's Springfield Park (the last ever competitive match to be played there) on Saturday 15 May. This was the first leg of the semi-final, with the second leg scheduled for the following Wednesday at Maine Road.

League form seems to count for nothing in these games, with four times out of the previous five seasons, the lowest qualifier for this League's Play-offs beating the highest placed qualifier.

The press made much of this in the build up to the match. Wigan had already won at Wembley just a few weeks before, winning the Football League Trophy. The run to the Final had built up their hefty games in hand bank, the majority of which they won to sneak into the Play-offs at the death.

This made them a form team and hungry to get back to Wembley quickly. The Play-offs and promotion would be a huge unexpected bonus for them while City and their fans were absolutely desperate to start the path back up the hierarchy.

The authors were wracked with nerves. It was another of those, 'we should win occasions', but of course supporting City had taught us never to expect too much. Jock would miss both legs due to injury too.

Will listened to the radio commentary. Listening to football on the radio can be purgatory. You cannot see what is happening and are totally reliant on the skill of the commentator.

They always pick up the obvious moments but often fail to spot runs off the ball as they concentrate on the man in possession. You feel like a blind man, often not knowing what is about to happen until it does. This makes you very nervy as you listen and that day Will was like the cat on a hot tin roof, pacing round and round the kitchen.

The game kicked off in front of fewer than 7,000 fans in Wigan's tiny condemned stadium. This was comfortably topped by 9,000 more who watched the game on a giant screen at City's Maine Road ground.

There was nothing comfortable about the start to the game from City's point of view. A horrendous mistake gifted Wigan the lead inside the first minute.

Messrs Reliable, Wiekens and Weaver left a defensive throw to each other and Wigan striker Barlow nipped in to roll the ball into an unguarded net.

Will banged the worktop as 9,000 City fans stared at the screen at City's home ground. Nobody believed it. The build up had raised expectations of a very tight contest, there would probably only be a goal in it and 20 seconds into the first leg City were already a goal down.

A sense of doom came over Will. Another season in this League, more games at Wycombe, at Colchester, at Oldham and at Chesterfield. To a large extent this season had been a novelty, a chance to visit new grounds, to see new cities and to truly be the big fish in a little pond.

To do it again would be a chore, old hat. How many fans would stay loyal for a second season?

As City spurned chance after chance, Will became increasingly desperate. He noted that the oven was electric and not gas!

Wigan came back into it and had a couple of very good chances themselves, Weaver saving well and the referee (future Premier League official Alan Wiley) waving away their penalty claims after Wiekens appeared to handle.

It is debatable whether City could have come back from two down but having survived those scares, we equalised in the 75th minute with a well-taken goal. The ball was crossed from the right and Dickov nipped in front of a defender to sweep the ball home from inside the area. 9,000 big screen watchers, 1,200 more inside the ground and a Croydon based fan confined to the kitchen, all went mad in perfect unison.

That's more like it! The game ended one apiece and Blue Moon rang out as the Wigan fans applauded their heroes and waved goodbye to their home. What a relief. We had taken a peep inside the abyss and turned our backs on it. Now we would be favourites for a Wembley day out. Will and Martyn would enjoy that.

It wasn't actually quite May when City met United in 2012, it was in fact the last day of April.

It was billed as the most important Manchester derby in history. Played 162 times since 1881, never had the derby been of such magnitude. The previous season's FA Cup semi-final paled into insignificance, as did the 1974 match when a Dennis Law back heel for City condemned his former club to relegation to Division Two, as did City's pivotal 3-1 victory at Old Trafford in March 1968 as City eventually went on to win their second and last League title.

This was to be winner takes all, the one that would sort the men from the boys and could shape the next 10 years for both clubs.

If City lost or drew, the title would go to United. Not definitely but almost certainly. If City won, we would be in pole position, it would be ours to lose. Both clubs were in the strange position of holding the destiny to the title in their own hands, just like in 1989 when Arsenal beat Liverpool in the final game to leapfrog the Merseysiders and take the title back to Highbury, spawning Nick Hornby's wonderful book, *Fever Pitch*.

The hype surrounding the 163rd Manchester derby was unbelievable. From the moment that City clinched that win at Wolves, the whole of the English media were focused on one thing only, the huge match at the Etihad.

The authors lapped it up like all the followers of both clubs. Conversations with friends and colleagues all referenced the contest. People who never talked about foootball were suddenly asking Will and Martyn for their opinion about what would happen in the game. The answer was always the same; it will be very tight, too close to call.

Will was actually quietly confident that City would win. He would not admit the fact to anyone for fear of kyboshing the Blues.

The authors failed to get tickets for what was a Monday night match. We had applied weeks in advance when there was actually the awful possibility of United actually clinching the title if they had got a result on the evening. Even with that ominous possibility, the game was still sold out weeks beforehand.

So Will and Martyn had to settle for sofa tickets in front of Sky's MNF coverage. Excellent coverage it was too.

Gary Neville used to be probably the most hated player at City (and Liverpool). He was United through and through and alongside Giggs and Scholes (both playing that night) he had personified the Red Devils for 16 seasons. Neville had antagonised City fans like no other.

His wild celebrations at the previous season's late late winner for United in the 4-3 League derby had seen him fined by the FA, and he was an unused substitute that day! He was probably more passionate about United than any other player and had been the top English right-back for well over a decade, winning 80 odd England caps and playing over 600 times for United during their golden period.

After his retirement as a player, Sky Sports soon unveiled him as their new football pundit in succession to the sacked Andy Gray. Upon the announcement there was an outcry among supporters of clubs other than United. He would be biased towards the Reds and anti City, Liverpool, Arsenal, Chelsea, etc.

Neville knew that he could not be, as difficult as it must have been to hide his United passion. He made his punditry debut analysing City's opening day win against Swansea. Although understandably nervous, he gave a very good analysis of the game, even managing to interview Roberto Mancini and congratulate him on a fine win while drooling over Kun Agüero's explosive debut.

He then went from strength to strength, so much so that he is now respected by City fans and all the rest.

His preview of the match was superb, the best preview that Will had ever seen. He described the match as the biggest in the 20-year Premier League history, laying on the line the effect that the result could have on both clubs. What if Tevez scored a late winner, what if Scholes did the same for United?

He then pinpointed the players and pivotal matches that had got us to this position. Agüero's finishing, the return of Tevez, the fantastic seasons enjoyed by Vinny and Yaya.

The 6-1 at Old Trafford, United's steely resolve in winning single goal victories, their Boxing Day defeat at home to Blackburn, City's defeats at Everton and Swansea, dropped points at home to Sunderland and the late comeback win against Chelsea.

United's loss of Vidic due to injury for the majority of the season and of course their defeat at Wigan and the 4-4 against Everton. If Evra's easy headed chance had gone in instead of staying out, that would probably have been it. Season over. A few millimetres had kept the season alive.

Neville even admitted that City were the better team that season with better players but United had the experience of winning titles and the resolve to do so again.

Having eaten, drank, breathed and slept with thoughts of the match for eight days, it was finally time to kick-off. Hundreds of millions watched worldwide. Will received good luck messages from Greece and Australia, Will and Martyn had probably exchanged 30 texts that day already.

Martyn watched the game at Los Angeles Airport on his way to Vegas. He was honeymooning with his new wife in the States and at 1pm the newlyweds took up their seats in a Mexican restaurant, the only venue in LAX that seemed to be showing the game. The sound was on mute but hey, beggars can't be choosers.

The atmosphere in the Etihad was fantastic (non-existent in LA!), this was a game like no other and the sell-out crowd wanted the win more badly than any other time. The noise level was cranked up several notches above the norm.

The first half was a typical derby, feisty tackling, full commitment but not much pretty stuff. United it seemed had come for the draw. They had set themselves up as hard to beat with attacking trio Welbeck, Young and Valencia all confined to the bench to allow for solid midfielder Park and experienced duo Giggs and Scholes. The result was a midfield battle for the most part.

The game seemed to be heading for goalless first half, when in the 45th minute City won a corner. Kompany lost his marker and thumped a header into the net. The joy was instant. Vinny wheeled away in vein-pumping exultation, the captain had broken the deadlock, leading by monumental example as he had done all season.

The place errupted, Will was physically unable to send a text, such were his emotions. The half-time whistle soon blew and the whole place was buzzing.

Over in California, Martyn had let out the most almighty yelp as the ball rocketed home. Every diner turned their head to see what the commotion was all about as the young Brit took centre stage.

A slightly blushing Martyn clenched his fist in triumph and the multi-national clientele broke out into a round of applause. Seems tourists are easily pleased in Tinseltown!

The second half was equally intense, Mancini and Ferguson even having a furious touchline row. In truth, United never looked like scoring and it turned out that the skipper's goal was enough for the three priceless points.

We had done it! Surely the title was ours. We just needed to keep the Lord Mayor at bay for two more games. No more typical City, PLEASE!!!!

With two games to play, we now topped the table on goal difference, eight goals to the good.

Team	P	W	D	L	F	A	GD	PTS
Manchester City	36	26	5	5	88	27	61	83
Manchester United	36	26	5	5	86	33	53	83

Thoughts immediately turned to the next game. City had a really difficult looking match at Champions League qualification chasing Newcastle while United had a comfortable looking home game against mid-table Swansea.

Beyond that United had an away game against mid-table Sunderland while City finished with a home game against a QPR side battling relegation and managed by Mancini's City predecessor, Mark Hughes.

Mancini said that United were still favourites. They had two easy games while we had two massive Cup Finals. Was he trying to galvanise Brendan Rodgers and Martin O'Neill, the managers of United's last two opponents, to inspire their troops to fight every inch of the way? We shall see...

On 19 May 1999 over 31,000 fans crammed into Maine Road for the second leg against Wigan. Just like the United derby of 2012, this North West version would be a tight affair. The first leg had shown that there was very little between the teams, City were favourites but that counted for nothing.

Will took up his position in the kitchen once more to listen on the radio. He was tense. All those thoughts of the abyss, of Adams Park, Layer Road, Boundary Park and Saltergate, of brass bands and wagon wheels, of uncompromising defenders and bully-boy centre-forwards, came flooding back. This was a massive 90 minutes, we just had to win!

The crowd and the players were tense too. The atmosphere was charged and the play frenetic. City were having slightly the better of it but Wigan had another very good shout for a penalty. We escaped again.

In the 25th minute City took the lead in controversial circumstances. Brown crossed from the right and poacher Goater bundled the ball home from close in.

But what part of his anatomy had he bundled the ball home with? Was it his hip, his stomach or his arm? The crowd went wild but Will lamented.

The radio commentator had advised that the goal would not stand, it had been disallowed for handball and Wigan had been awarded a free-kick. But wait a minute, it did stand after all and as the Wigan players protested, Will went on a delayed run of celebration around his kitchen. 'Feed the Goat and he will score!'

Wigan pressed for an equaliser from then on. The tension grew as the game opened up as it wore on, with Wigan attacking and City defending desperately.

Six minutes from time, Wigan were awarded a free-kick just outside the area. It was one of those unbearable moments as the defensive wall was prepared and the Wigan attackers discussed which training ground routine to apply. Will, hands in pockets, walked round and round in circles chanting, 'No! No! No! No! No!' repeatedly.

He listened mesmerised as the whistle blew. The cross came in, the striker rose, 'it's off the bar!' shrieked the commentator, 'it's still not clear…it is now and City survive a major scare.'

Will breathed a huge sigh of relief. Football is some pastime! Wigan continued to press in the dying minutes but as they threw men forwards, they were vulnerable to counter-attacks. Three times in the last few minutes City had great chances to kill the game off but fluffed them all.

Then, after what seemed an age, the referee blew the final whistle. We had done it and were going to Wembley. The fans rushed onto the pitch to congratulate their heroes while Will phoned his nephew.

'That was absolute agony, I hated every minute of it. Now we are at Wembley and should be able to get tickets as Gillingham have beaten Preston and they have fewer fans. Thanks goodness that's all over, I don't think I could have taken much more!'

Rania's Christmas present in 2011 was a short spring break in Paris. As it panned out it would coincide with City's penultimate league game of the 11/12 season, away at Newcastle.

The match would be played on Sunday lunchtime, and as luck would have it, this meant that there was just time to take in the match before dashing for the Eurostar.

Will had it all planned. He located an Irish bar right next door to the Moulin Rouge. The game would finish about 45 minutes from the Eurostar departure time and a taxi dash would get them there just in time.

Will will deny the fact that his wife's special weekend was in any way spoiled by the impending momentous game, but he will admit that it was dominating his thoughts.

His mind would wander as he watched cool jazz; the Mona Lisa reminded him of a moody City fan, a magpie in Jardin des Tuileries had obvious connotations (Newcastle's nickname is the Magpies), the Crazy Horse Cabaret reminded him of ex-Liverpool and England defender Emlyn Hughes (whose nickname was Crazy Horse), which reminded him of football, which reminded him of the game. To be truthful, no reminders were really necessary. This was City's biggest away game for years and years, only Wigan in

'99 came close in the last 40 years. Will reminded Martyn by text that the last time City won the title in '68, we clinched first place by winning the last game 4-3 at Newcastle at the same time that Sunderland were winning at Old Trafford. We won the League that season by two points, could that be an omen with those same North East opponents significant again?

Will put a tenner on City to win 4-3 at 66-1 just in case.

Sunday morning seemed to drag somewhat. We were staying in bohemian Montmartre. After a nice relaxing brunch and a stroll around Sacré Coeur there were still two hours until kick-off. Will had already checked that the game would be shown at Sullivans Bar but he decided to check again. It used up 20 minutes waiting time and gave the second confirmation, just in case it were needed.

At last it was time to take our seats in the bar. There were multi-screens and the bar was virtually empty. After frustrating his good lady wife by try-ing every vantage point possible, Will eventually chose where we would sit for the game.

Will's stomach was in knots. He had been nervous for the United game but this game took the nerves to another level. Newcastle had got a fabulous win at Chelsea in midweek to put them in pole position for fourth spot and Champions League qualification.

Their Senegalise striker Cissé had scored a wonder goal in that game that was to eclipse Crouch's strike against City for goal of the season. Will texted Martyn, 'at least he has got that goal now, he couldn't do it again, surely'.

The players came out for the pre-match handshakes and Sky TV cut to the adverts. The first advert shown was one for Peugeot, nothing remarkable about that you would think. However, much of the artwork that appeared in the advert had been designed and produced by Kyle, another nephew of Will's. This was taken as a lucky omen.

When the game kicked off, Will was soon kicking every ball, squirming in his seat and forgetting he was in public, such was his height of animation. The bar had a few more in now, including a couple of Aussies who had picked up on Will's partizan support and decided it would be fun to vociferously back Newcastle.

Newcastle had a shot that flew miles wide, the Aussies gasped loudly. City had a shot that went close, the Aussies shouted 'wide', as if they were cricket umpires.

Will fumed and wished they would shut up. When Yaya committed a foul that deservedly earned a yellow card, the Aussies (and 50,000 Geordies) cried, 'Send him off!'

Will had enough of such garbage. 'Do you know the rules of football?' he shouted across the bar. Rania cringed but luckily for Will the Aussies were lacking the famed caustic wit that Antipodeans are well known for. The rather meek reply was, 'it was a bad foul'.

'Yes it was a yellow card foul and that is what he has got.' End of conversation. Thankfully.

Will could now concentrate again on the last hour of what was an absorbing contest. At 0-0 and with less than half an hour to go, the tension was starting to get palpable in Newcastle and Paris. Will was again forgetting that he was in public with plenty of exclamation and the odd stifled expletive.

Mancini made his move, substituting attacking midfielder Nasri for defensive midfielder Nigel de Jong. This was a baffling decision for the uninitiated. Surely City needed goals and on the face of it this was a defence minded change.

The initiated of course knew the plan. The introduction of the Dutch anchorman freed Yaya from his defensive duties and allowed him to move his considerable frame more into the attacking third of the field.

The move took precisely eight minutes to pay off. Yaya exchanged passes with Kun before steering the ball past the goalkeeper and into the right-hand corner of the goal.

Will lost himself, standing up in his stool, arms aloft and simply shouting, 'YESSSSSSSS!!'

Just a few minutes later, Ageuro broke free to put City…but oh no, he placed his shot wide with the goal at his mercy. Rania slapped Will's leg as he forgot to stifle the expletive!

Newcastle then had a couple of decent chances to equalise and deal a fatal blow to City's title hopes. It was also dealing a blow to Will's blood pressure.

City survived however and in the last minute Yaya scored again, finishing a great breakaway after City had defended a corner.

Will lost it again, standing up in his stool, arms aloft once more and this time bellowing, 'get in the net, you fu**ing beauty!!!!!!!!' Another slap, but he didn't care.

At the end of the game City stood three points clear and now just needed Swansea to pull off an improbable victory at Old Trafford that afternoon and the title would be theirs.

There was just time for the Aussies to sportingly congratulate Will, before he and Rania grabbed their belongings, hailed a taxi and made the train with five minutes to spare. Rania does have to put up with a lot, when it comes to Will's love of football!

Will's phone beeped into text action as the train exited the tunnel back into England. United had won 2-0 and next Sunday would be the climax. Wow!!

Super Super Sundays

Sunday is supposed to be a day of rest. Church in the morning, a family roast dinner, leisurely afternoon pursuits, a nice bath, a period drama on the telly and then off to bed.

For as long as the authors can remember, Sunday has been a big sporting day. The Grand Prix, the Wimbledon Men's tennis final, Test Match Sunday (often the pivotal day), the World Cup Final, Six Nations Rugby and Sky's Super Sunday football double header.

A far cry from the days of Will's teenage years when all you got was John Player League Cricket and Ski Sunday – the day was the most boring of the week.

In 1999 and 2012 Sunday was to be Manchester City's day of destiny. Winner takes all, loser takes nothing days, no margin for error days, unbearably nerve wracking, gut wrenching, all encompassing mental agony days. In both years City were very hot favourites. In '99 it was the Nationwide

Division Two Play-off Final at Wembley against Gillingham, in 2012 it was the final League match of the season with City playing QPR at the Etihad Stadium, where they simply had to match or better Manchester United's result away at Sunderland to clinch their first ever Premier League Title.

With favouritism came expectation, which in turn brought huge pressure.

1999 was supposed to be the authors' big day out at Wembley. That was until the football authorities intervened.

The clubs would be allocated an equal number of tickets. That meant that City who had averaged around 28,000 during the season would get the same number of tickets as Gillingham who had averaged fewer than 10,000.

Whatever way Will turned, he was thwarted in his attempts to secure tickets for he and Martyn. He tried the City Supporters' Clubs of London and South West, the club itself, friends and acquaintances, but nothing.

These were the days before the Internet had really taken off as a sales room and Will was not exactly flush so could not afford hundreds of pounds for a ticket.

Will resigned himself to the fact that they would need to be with the Gillingham fans for the day. With a South London address, it shouldn't be difficult to get tickets from Kent's only club, even if he would have to take out membership as well.

A call to Gillingham dashed this, however, Gillingham had sold out too! Will cannot remember the exact numbers but thinks that maybe each club got 35,000 tickets with another 5,000 or so being available to neutrals, sponsors, dignitaries etc.

This meant that Gillingham got over three times their average gate while City barely covered their season ticket holders!

The upshot of this was that two City fans as obsessed with City as any other, who had followed City to York, Wycombe, Bournemouth and others that season, who had been a season ticket holder in the past, who had witnessed City's relegation nadir the previous season, who had a 23-year-old City mirror hung in their hallway as well as a silk scarf, who owned 2,000 City programmes and had meticulously kept City scrapbooks in their youth, may not be able to see the game.

In contrast, any granny, any great aunt, anybody with the slightest interest in football, anybody without the slightest interest in football, in fact just about one third of Gillingham's entire population could go to the game, even if they had not attended a match during this or any other season!

Was that fair? I suppose you could argue that City having three times as many fans there as their opponents would make it like a City home game and give an unfair advantage. Point taken, but at the time Will and nephew thought it ridiculous.

Will told Martyn not to worry. There would surely be lots of spare tickets on the day. Plenty of Kentish mums and sisters who decided shopping was preferable after all. The pair decided to get to Wembley early to make sure they had the best chance of picking up tickets.

Armed with home made signs stating, '2 TICKETS NEEDED AT REASONABLE PRICE', we arrived at 10am, five hours before kick-off. We must have walked miles as we tried to find those elusive tickets. The only enquiries that our signs brought were 'are you selling?' Can't you bloody well read, no we NEED TO BUY tickets!

That is what we thought rather than said, as most of the enquiries came from City fans struck with the same curse as us, that is the curse of being ticketless, not the curse of supporting City!

As midday turned to one o'clock we were getting desperate and resorted to acting like touts, 'anybody got any spare tickets?' we uttered. As time wore on and we became even more desperate our volume increased. We even asked Barry Fry, he of jovial football management fame and there as a media pundit, if he could get us in! 'No chance lads,' he chuckled back.

By two o'clock we had given up. In four hours of being at Wembley we had not seen one ticket changing hands. Most fans were already inside the stadium lapping up the atmosphere or buying some exorbitantly priced beers.

On one of our circumferences of the stadium, we had noticed a pub and decided we would head there to see if they were showing the game. On entering the pub we were extremely grateful to see that the Sky coverage was indeed being shown.

We would watch the game and when (IF) City won, we would rush back to the stadium and join the post match celebrations. If we were really lucky we would gain admittance as the disappointed Gillingham fans and the non-partizan day-trippers left in their droves.

At 2.30pm the screen switched over to the Eastenders omnibus. A dash to the bar and we were to face disappointment again. Apparently local licensing laws prohibited pubs within a close proximity to Wembley Stadium from showing any match taking place there.

OMG, City's biggest game in decades and two of their loyal followers were going to miss at least some of it!

A plan was hatched; we would get to Central London as soon as possible and watch the match in the Sports Café in Haymarket.

We legged it to Wembley Train Station. Luckily there was a train to Marylebone within a few minutes. From there we took the Bakerloo Line to Piccadilly Circus from where we dodged the traffic to rush to the bar.

We arrived breathless (at least Will was!) just as they kicked off. The last five hours had been so desperate and then so eventful, that we had forgotten our nerves. They soon kicked in again.

Clutching a largely untouched bottle of beer, the Blues decked in City attire, watched the game unfold. It was very tight. Chances were few and far between in the first half. There was so much at stake that attractive football was definitely not the order of the day. For anybody that knows the Sports Café you will be aware that it is a real magnet for tourists. It shows all kinds of sports, with different events showing in different areas of the vast bar and restaurant. Knowing that it was a tourist venue, you will not be surprised to learn that there were a few United fans lurking.

The Red idiots, latched onto our City gear and proceeded to take the mickey out of City and cheer on Gillingham for the entire 45 minutes. This irked the authors no end, so much so that they hotfooted it up Haymarket to watch the rest of the match in the now defunct Football Football.

The second half became far more open. Goater was unlucky to see his header hit the post and there seemed to be a lot more gaps opening up as the game wore on and defences tired on Wembley's expansive turf.

Extra-time was looming as the clock turned past 80 minutes. Then disaster struck. Gillingham penetrated the City rearguard and suddenly Gills striker Carl Asaba found himself in the clear. As Weaver rushed out to block, Asaba steered the ball over his head and into the net.

Football Football suddenly became very noisy. Clearly we were the only City fans there and the neutrals watching favoured the Southern underdogs. We were gutted of course.

Almost immediately City had a great chance to equalise but Dickov's low close range shot was blocked by the leg of Gillingham 'keeper Vince Bartram, who just so happened to have been the best man at Dickov's wedding! They had played together in Arsenal's youth team.

Four minutes later and catastrophe. A Gillingham goal-kick was controlled and then back-heeled by Asaba into the path of his on-rushing strike partner Bob Taylor. Taylor drilled a low shot from outside the area, past Weaver's left hand and inside his post. We were 2-0 down with 86 minutes up on the clock.

Martyn and Will looked at each other, speechless with tears welling up. We had taken a look at the abyss but this time had fallen spellbound into its bowels. The Lord Mayor had spoken. City would not be promoted. Again we would be playing in the third tier, another tough 46 games to try and start the long climb back to respectability.

The Goat would leave, Weaver would be snapped up by a higher division club, Wiekens too and Cooke would be sold as soon as we had signed him (we secured the permanent transfer in April for £1 million to secure his Play-off participation). The great Ian Bishop would retire with his head bowed. How depressing.

We did not hear whether anybody cheered. We were in our own miserable world, oblivious to the commentator's words, just staring blankly at the screen, our thoughts were only focused on our failure, we could not even summon the words to ask each other if we should leave.

The Gallaghers of Oasis fame did just that. They could stand no more and were pictured leaving their Wembley box behind them. This was not rock and roll, this was the blues at its most melancholic.

Co-commentator Brian Horton, who once managed City in the Premier League, said it all, 'that's game over, that's killed the game off now'.

The game moved into the 90th minute. The ball broke to Kevin Horlock just outside the penalty area and he directed a precise shot through a crowd of players and into the net. There was a muted cheer at Wembley, the authors did not even bother to do that. Typical of City to get a late consolation, enough to just give us slight hope only to have those hopes cruelly dashed. Many City fans had followed the Gallaghers example and left early.

A few decided to come back on hearing that cheer, just in time to hear a huge roar of encouragement from the City faithful as the reserve referee held up a board showing that there would be five minutes of injury time.

We couldn't do it surely? With barely a minute left on the clock, Gerard Wiekens played a long ball into the box and big Gareth Taylor, on as a sub, flicked it on and the ball found its way to the Goat via Horlock's neat lay-off. The Goat's shot was blocked but the ball broke free to Paul Dickov, inside the area. Then time stood still. Dicky with his back to goal controlled the ball, swivelled around and moved it forward slightly, as a Gillingham defender dived in desperately. The wee Scot then skillfully lifted the ball over the sliding defender and the head of his best man and into the back of the net.

City had done it! The great escape act. City fans inside the stadium and Football Football went absolutely nuts. A season's worth of emotion let out in one mesmeric, incredible, unbelievable, orgasmic moment of pure ecstasy.

Will and Martyn hugged each other, jumping up and down as if they were at a Sex Pistols gig, 34-year-old uncle and his 17-year-old nephew, united in joy, all of the demons of the abyss exorcised in a single wonderful instant.

There was hardly time to re-start before the final whistle blew. City had only earned 30 minutes of extra-time but the feeling was that we had won. The pleasure of those two late goals gave the winning feeling by themselves, but surely with City on such a high and with Gillingham at such a contrasting draining, almost debilitating low, all the momentum was with City.

We thought it would be a formality from now on, especially as Gillingham had subbed Asaba, their most dangerous striker as they looked to protect their precious lead.

The City players celebrated like they had won it and we did too.

Extra-time ended up being just a slog. Both teams were emotionally and physically drained and neither could muster what you would term as a real chance.

Referee Halsey (also destined to referee in the Premier League) blew for the end of extra-time. The match was to be decided on penalties.

The lottery of penalties to finish the lottery of the Play-offs. We had witnessed the penalty heartaches of Italia '90 and Euro '96 – who would be the Waddle or the Southgate this time?

Will was strangely confident. We still had the momentum despite the 30 minutes of stalemate. We had lost for all intents and purposes but now here we were with a stay of execution and another chance of victory.

As always, it seems to take an age to start the shoot-out. The end the penalties will be taken needs to be sorted (the City supporters' end on this occasion – a definite advantage and another cause for optimism), the referee needs to know the order of the penalty takers, including the order of takers 6-11 if there is no result after five penalties each, a coin is tossed to see which team will take the first kick.

All this delay enabled the Gallaghers to sneak back in time to witness the drama.

Finally up stepped Super Kevin Horlock to score with ease. 1-0 City!

Next up Gills midfielder Paul Smith. He didn't look confident as the City masses jeered constantly. He shot low down the middle of the goal but Weaver guessed correctly and saved with his legs. Still 1-0 City!

Up stepped goal hero Paul Dickov. Surely it was his day. He hit the ball low and hard, it hit the base of the post to his right, rolled along the line and off the other post. Unbelievably he had missed. Still 1-0 City! This was agonising to watch.

It was Gillingham defender Adrian Pennock's turn next. He shot woefully wide. Four penalties gone and still 1-0 City! Incredible but still our advantage.

Terry Cooke looked extremely confident as he stepped up and rightly so as he tucked it away with aplomb. 2-0 City!

John Hodge stepped up next. Will had once sung his name while he played for his second favourite team Exeter City, 'Johnny Hodge, Johnny Hodge, flying down the wing', to the tune of the *Robin Hood* theme song. Surely he will miss it for us. No, excellent spot-kick. 2-1 City!

So who's next? Oh no, not Richard Edghill! Our left-back was not known for his scoring prowess. In nearly 100 League games he had not troubled the goalscorer statisticians.

Was this wise? We collectively held our breath. He fired his shot high, we finally exhaled in relief as it went in via the underside of the bar. 3-1 City!

Gillingham now needed to score this next penalty to prolong the contest. Up stepped defender Guy Butters. We held our breath again. His spot kick was to Weaver's left but the 'keeper dived the right way to make the save. 3-1 City and we had won!

This sparked scenes of unbridled joy at Wembley and one football themed Central London bar. It was like we had won twice in one day.

The players celebrated wildly. Nicky Weaver went on a legendary run, doing a sporting impression of Duncan Norville's chase me.

Jock Morrison was the first to catch him, virtually rugby tackling him to the floor leading to all the other players diving on top like a school playground game of crush.

Back at the bar, the result and what it meant was starting to sink in. The best players would stay, we would sign some more quality, we would be visiting some half decent stadiums, most importantly we would be only one promotion away from the Premier League.

What a relief. Could we have turned the corner?

After the game, the authors ordered two glasses of over priced and poor quality champagne to toast the success. In reality this was just symbolic, something to acknowledge our victory from the jaws of defeat.

After a couple of sips we decided to head to Covent Garden as we assumed that was the area that would be a magnet for City fans post Wembley. They never materialised and thinking about it, we should have headed for the Marylebone/Baker Street area, which would have been a natural stop off on the way back to Euston.

Never mind, at least a few Scandinavian tourists congratulated us, one of whom claimed to be a City fan but thought that Uwe Rosler still played for us and that Kare Ingebrigsten had been a good player!

On the journey back to Croydon, Will reminded Martyn of our Torpoint adventure all those months ago. Gerard Wiekens had been our quiz team colleague that day and Will had said to him that getting back to the Premiership in two years had to be our aim. Wiekens had just shrugged his shoulders and replied, 'we will try'.

Part one accomplished.

That was also the first chapter in our Superior Super Sundays double mission.

Bringing us right back to the here and now, Queen's Park Rangers were the 2012 opponents, The Etihad Stadium, our home since 2003, was the venue.

This was the moment that we had been waiting for all those years. We remembered the games at York and Wycombe, we remembered Wembley '99, we remembered being lower than Crewe, Stockport and Bury, we remembered the relegations and missed opportunities, we remembered the woefully inadequate players that had worn the sacred blue of City.

This was the day that we would exorcise all the years of suffering, 40+ years of hurt never stopped us dreaming.

City had survived 'squeaky bum time' really well. Fergie's mind games had fallen on deaf ears, Mancini being masterful at ignoring the bait and simply responding what a great team United were and that we just aspired to be something like them.

For the first time he actually admitted that the title was ours to lose. He was confident that we would deliver.

QPR were all that stood in our way. They had the worst away scoring record in the League (17 goals in 18 games) while Sunderland had been the only opponents to leave The Etihad with anything at all when we drew 3-3 in April. On any normal day this would be a walkover.

But it was far from ordinary, the title outcome rested on the result for City, while QPR were in a straight dogfight with Bolton for the last relegation place. If QPR lost and Bolton won at Stoke, Rangers would be heading straight back to the Championship.

To add spice to the occasion, QPR were managed by City's former manager and former United star Mark Hughes. Fergie had helpfully mentioned at every press conference that week that City had treated Hughes terribly. He was probably right, but did he really think that Hughes needed any more incentive to take points off us?

In fact the entire QPR management team had all been sacked by City with Hughes. Plenty of grudges there then.

In addition Rangers' captain was none other than former City tearaway Joey Barton. Barton had left the club in 2007 under a cloud after assaulting teammate Ousmane Dabo during training. This had been the final straw in a string of misdemeanours and he was packed off to Newcastle for £5 million.

Also in the QPR ranks was Nedum Onuoha, who had joined them in the January transfer window. It was Nedum's mother who had been notoriously ridiculed by former City chief executive Garry Cooke in a leaked email. This led to Cooke resigning and had left a bitter taste in Onuoha's mouth, despite the fact that he had been at City since being a schoolboy.

Finally there was Shaun Wright-Phillips, one of City's favourite sons from the past 20 years, who had moved to London on transfer deadline day the previous summer. Shaun still loved City and especially City's fans. He had admitted publicly that part of his heart would always be sky blue on the day he officially left us for the second time. He stated now that his perfect day would be for City to be crowned champions and QPR to survive.

City's only rivals for the title were of course near neighbours Manchester United, who were expected to win comfortably at Sunderland, meaning that City would have to win too.

Mancini had tried to rouse Sunderland by stating this was an easy fixture for United. This did annoy Martin O'Neill, Sunderland's manager and an ex-City midfielder. He obviously only cared about Sunderland and isn't the type of manager to accept anything other than 100%, no matter what the occasion.

Not only had Sunderland taken more points off City than any other team that season, but had also lost 1-0 at Old Trafford courtesy of an own goal by ex-United defender Wes Brown!

Sunderland also had three other ex-United players in their squad, defenders John O'Shea and Phil Bardsley and striker Fraser Campbell.

There were enough sub plots for a Frederick Forsyth novel!

The build up to the big day had been intense. Will's text and email inbox together with his Facebook pages and Twitter feed had gone into overdrive. Every neutral seemed to want a City win, even though we had spent hundreds of millions to get in the position we were now in.

People were bored with United winning the biggest football prize in England. For most it was anybody but United will do. Even the media, so often accused of being pro United, now seemed to be welcoming the winds of change.

This was the 20th anniversary season of the Premier League and the 2011-12 season had already been officially voted the best ever, and there was still more to come.

Will and Martyn re-enacted much of the 2011 FA Cup Final ritual. Flags out, ribbons on dog, Blue Moon beer.

Martyn arrived from his Brighton home 90 minutes before kick-off. The greeting hug was a little warmer than usual, this was a special day, this was our day, the day that we like every other City fan had dreamed of for years but in truth had never expected to happen.

Martyn had recently been joined in marriage but we were joined in City, a bond almost as deep as man and wife's, probably more so for many.

We lapped up Sky's pre-match coverage and felt the hairs stand up on the backs of our necks as the TV showed Vinny's header flying into the United net. The week before the big day had dragged by but time fled once Martyn arrived and it was soon time for kick-off. We wished each other luck as if we were about to take our driving test and made ourselves comfortable for the ride.

City were unchanged from the Newcastle game, except for Mario returning to take a place on the bench.

City started tentatively, the nerves had had an effect. Those nerves were reflected on the terraces and certainly in Will's lounge.

Thirteen minutes in and the first important goal of the day had been scored. Stoke were beating Bolton 1-0. The QPR fans cheered wildly, they and the players could breathe a little easier.

Not long afterwards, there was a goal at Sunderland's Stadium of Light. A small screen was inserted into the main screen showing our match and the replay confirmed straight away that it was a goal for United.

The City fans groaned, the Rangers fans unsportingly cheered once more. The tension in the stands was ramped up a few more notches and this translated itself onto the pitch.

City were playing nowhere near their fluent best. Misplaced passes, snatched attempts on goal and the defending was definitely of the ruffled variety. The authors squirmed uneasily in their seats. It quickly seemed to be turning into one of those days that we did not look like scoring. Just one please, just one!

Just as we were thinking get in to half-time so Mancini can work his motivational magic, we got one after 39 minutes, Pablo Zabaleta choosing the momentous occasion to score his first goal of the season after a great pass by Yaya. The authors shouted at the top of their voices, relief as much as anything. The goal would calm the nerves and we could go back to normal service and a comfortable win.

Unfortunately the inspirational Yaya soon left the fray due to injury to be replaced by De Jong. There would be no plan B today but we were not that worried, we would be OK.

So it was as you were at half-time with both clubs with Manchester in their name winning a goal to nil. For QPR however it was not so good. Bolton were now leading at Stoke and if the scores remained the same, it would be the R's and not the Trotters that would be relegated.

The City fans politely chanted, 'going down, going down, going down'. Well all's fair in love and war as they say!

Three minutes into the second half, that all changed and it was not good news for City. Shaun Wright-Phillips knocked a hopeful ball forward, the usually reliable Joleon Lescott fluffed his attempt at a back header and Djibril Cisse latched onto it and drilled a low hard shot past Joe Hart.

As the commentator helpfully explained that as it stood United were champions, the authors sunk into their seats. 'What the f**k was Lescott doing?' shrieked Will, 'an assist from SWP,' Martyn matter of factly replied.

The small screen re-appeared showing United's celebrating fans. They were still winning.

Now we were back to square one. The crowd were anxious, the players were anxious and the authors were most definitely anxious. Surely we are not going to blow it right at the death. After all we have been through.

A crazy few minutes that only Joey Barton could have conjured completely changed our perspective and mood.

We had missed it but the commentator explained, 'Tevez is down holding his face after a clash with Barton just outside the penalty area.'

The referee blew his whistle. Replays showed a coming together between the perpetrators, arms flapping from both before Barton clearly aimed an elbow at Tevez. 'He's got to go, send the bast**d off, send him off, he's got to go,' Will bellowed.

Sure enough, red was shown and QPR were down to 10 men. He refused to go quietly, first of all kneeing Kun Agüero in the back of his thigh, then aiming a headbutt at Kompany and remonstrating with Mario before a combination of Micah Richards and the QPR coaching staff ushered him off.

'It was like a drunk being thrown out of a club,' remarked Will, 'I have given him the benefit of the doubt in the past but that is unforgivable.'

Back to the action. There were 35 minutes to go and with QPR down to 10 men, now it was time to make our numerical and ability advantage count.

Hughes took off scorer Cisse and replaced him with defender Traore. They would try and defend their point that would keep them safe and hand the title to United. 'Why couldn't we be playing someone safely in mid table?' lamented Will. 'It is ours now,' responded Martyn.

The handily placed free-kick had come to nothing and QPR were clearly intent in defending en masse. City would need some ingenuity to unlock the barrier before them.

On 66 minutes QPR broke free from their shackles. Traore galloped down the left, sped past Zabaleta and sent in a cross towards the on rushing Jamie Mackie. Will used to sing Mackie's name when he played for his second favourite team, Exeter City, surely he would miss? No, a brilliant downward diving header evaded Hart and Lescott and bounced once into the net. GOAL!!!!

Ten-man QPR were now winning against all the odds. Our world had caved in. We were desperate. The small screen made its entrance, jubilant United fans at Sunderland. F**K OFF!!!!!

We looked like our ideas had run out. Virtually total possession but no clue on how to pick the massed defence. Džeko came on for Barry and Mario for the tiring and largely ineffective Tevez.

Džeko hit a post, Mario brought a great save out of Kenny. We pressed and pressed and pressed but no way through.

Close to tears, the authors sat in stunned silence, staring blankly at the screen. It just wasn't happening, we were resigned to our dismal fate.

United were still winning, their fans chanting, 'Champions, Champions, Champions.'

We were running out of ideas and time. Corner after corner came to nothing. With only five minutes remaining, Will turned off his mobile. He couldn't stomach any commiserations or worse still gloating United fans.

'I don't think I can recover from this,' Will mournfully whispered. He has no idea whether Martyn responded, he was now in an almost comatose state. All he could think of was Fergie dancing across the Sunderland pitch, of Ferdinand and Scholes and Rooney celebrating in front of their ecstatic fans.

He imagined walking into the office the next day. He would have to phone in sick.

City kept plugging away, scrambles, final passes not finding their man, Kenny standing firm, defenders making last ditch tackles. Oh how we could have done with one of Yaya's bulldozing runs. Why! Why! Why! Why!

Typical City, The Lord Mayor, The Maine Road Gypsy's Curse, all back to haunt us with a vengeance.

The fourth official held up the board. Five minutes of injury time. Those that remembered Gillingham '99 mustered half a roar of encouragement but soon quietened down again when they realised we needed two goals in stoppage time, not the one goal that Dickov had delivered 13 years before.

We were out for the count, trying desperately but needing a miracle. QPR had all 10 men in the defensive third of the field and they were not budging.

When after 91 minutes, City won yet another corner, there was barely a stir. We must have been in this position 15 times in the second half alone. The cross from Silva came over and Džeko rose to head the ball home. GOAL!!!

City fans celebrated. Not a word from the authors. This was just toying with us.

The volume increased, the fans were urging City forward, Mancini, who had been going demented on the touchline all afternoon, gesticulated. FORWARD, FORWARD, FORWARD!!

At about this time the final whistles went at Sunderland and Stoke. United players went to salute their fans, confident that they were champions but not sure. At Stoke the game had finished 2-2, Bolton were relegated and QPR would be safe no matter what happened in the final two minutes in Manchester. They could relax, wish we could!

The ball was cleared by QPR once more. Nasri let the ball run for a throw in, unaware that it had clipped a City player on the way out. F**K!!!!!

The authors still had not moved, they were mesmerised. Then all of a sudden Agüero was in the box with the ball at his feet. Will had no idea how he had arrived at that moment; it was all a bit of a blur. Kun poked the ball nearer the goal, avoiding Nedum's desperate lunge.

In a flash, he despatched a firmly struck shot past Kenny's left hand. The net bulged. AGÜERO!!!!!!!!!!!! GOAL!!!!!! THEY'VE DONE IT!!!!!!!! CITY ARE CHAMPIONS!!!!!!!!!!!

YEEEESSSSSSSSSSSSS!!!!!!!!!!!!!!!!

The roar from the Etihad could be heard in Salford, the roar from Surrey could be heard in Kent. We had done it! We have won! The Title is ours! United have lost it!

Yes!!!!!!!!!!!!!!!!!!!!!!!!!!!! We are the Champions.

Will and Martyn both jumped up simultaneously and just hugged each other and sobbed. Not sure whether it was a lifetime of hurt or just 90 minutes of hell but we just cried. Tears of joy rather than the tears of failure that had been gathering for the last 10 minutes at least.

Never in just about any other facet of life could you experience so many emotions in less than two hours.

Expectation followed by concern followed by hope followed by joy followed by pain followed by frustration followed by despair followed by misery followed by hope followed by complete unadulterated orgasmic unbridled ecstasy.

There was still a minute to go but QPR did not care anymore. They were safe. Perhaps they had safely relaxed and that had allowed City in. Maybe. Rangers knocked the ball forward into no man's land, Hart collected and then the referee blew for time.

That was when the celebrations started in earnest. The crowd were on the pitch, the players were going bananas, Mancini, Platt, Kidd all going crazy, the substitutes and youth players bounding around like kangaroos. Absolute bedlam.

Liam Gallagher had stayed this time for it all! We were all rolling with it, experiencing a mass champagne supernova and definitely not looking back in anger!

It took 15 or 20 minutes to restore order. Will hugged Martyn, then he hugged his wife, then he hugged his dog. The champagne cork was popped. Will then switched on his mobile phone. 28 messages!

We gloated over the scenes at Sunderland. The woman celebrating United's title, then hearing the roar from the Black Cat fans, then the awful truth dawning on her. Silly cow!

Fergie trying to look contrite in defeat. Absolutely priceless!

Eventually the pitch cleared. Former greats and members of City's last League triumph, Mike Summerbee and Skipper Tony Book, brought on the Premier League Trophy, accompanied by other former players from the last Golden era such as Francis Lee and Glyn Pardoe.

The current players received their medals, Vinny took hold of the trophy and held it aloft as streamers and firecrackers exploded around him.

Manchester City Are Champions!

After The Lord Mayor's Show?

How do you follow those two roller-coaster rides of emotion? How do you avoid coming back down to earth with a bump? You look forward of course. Park the celebrations where they belong on the end of season DVD, learn from the experience and do it all again. And some.

So what happened after 1999? We definitely partied (as Prince suggested in his hit song), but then it was down to hard graft and finding a few quid to strengthen for the higher League.

In came Mark Kennedy for over £1 million from Wimbledon, £1 million full-back Danny Granville from Leeds, Tony Grant from Everton and Lee Peacock from Mansfield for £500,000 each and Big Bob Taylor arrived from vanquished Gillingham for £1.5 million. Latterly Spencer Prior, another beast of a centre-back like Jock, was bought to add some more steel to the defence.

Michael Brown was the first of the Wembley heroes to leave when he joined Sheffield United in the January.

Stunningly we mounted a serious promotion challenge, never leaving the top few places all season.

The authors went to a few games – the goalless draw at Fulham where Jock was sent off for licking Stan Collymore springs to mind as does a real hammering at Wolves.

The most memorable match attended was at Grimsby's Blundell Park in mid April. First of all the drive up seemed to go on for ever and although it was true that the town stinks of fish, the fish and chips were wonderful.

There were loads of City fans that day and we were all in great voice at a local pub. When we arrived at the ground at 2.30, there was a massive queue already to get in the City end.

They only had one turnstile open and as more and more fans turned up fuelled by beer, it started to get pretty hairy for a while. Sense finally prevailed and they opened two more entrances but by the time we got into the ground, they had already kicked off.

Grimsby were clearly not used to a large away following and although there were only just over 8,000 there, the place was bulging at the seams.

Bizarrely, we had to walk along the touchline and behind the goal to take our place in the terraces. We were pitch level en route to the stand when a free-kick was thumped home by the head of Spencer Prior after six minutes. It was like we were right in the action as the jubilant City players celebrated next to us.

The game finished one apiece – it was our first sighting of Prior in a City shirt and as well as scoring he looked completely dominant in the air. We did wonder whether he had an angled head though as many of his clearing headers seemed to go off at strange trajectories!

Will watched the season's penultimate game on the Greek island of Spetses with his Greek fiancée and his parents, there for a wedding year Easter break. The local bar had an illegal Sky Sports feed so Bob's your uncle.

In fact it was Bob's the only scorer, with Big Fat Bob Taylor (as he was affectionately known) settling a tense and scrappy affair at Maine Road against Birmingham.

This meant that on the final day City needed to win at Blackburn to condemn Ipswich to the Play-offs. If Ipswich won at home to Walsall and City lost, it would be City facing the lottery for the second year running.

The day was sunny and the mood upbeat. We had far exceeded all expectations and thanks to some excellent play all round and the Goat's 28 League goals, we were sitting pretty.

At half-time, it was the nightmare scenario that we faced. Ipswich led and City were one down. So dominant were Blackburn that they had hit the woodwork twice as well!

The authors watched the game at the now defunct Terry Neill's Bar on Holborn Viaduct. Like last year we had failed to get tickets for our biggest game but unlike 12 months before, this bar was full of City. The pre-match optimism had faded somewhat. Will's Ipswich supporting brother texted to gloat. A tad premature Will thought as he deleted it.

The second half started in the same vein as the first with Blackburn rattling the City woodwork twice more. Someone high up was watching over us that day – perhaps Peter Swales had pulled some strings with the Governor!

After an hour, Mark Kennedy broke clear and sent in a low cross, which the Goat converted for goal number 29. Feed the Goat and indeed he will score!

A point would be enough and the City fans went wild at Ewood Park, on a hillside vantage point above Ewood Park and at Terry's gaff.

Twenty minutes later and it was all over, City were incredibly 4-1 up and back in the big time. Fittingly Dicky, the Wembley goalscoring hero from 1999, got the fourth.

So back in the Big Time and Will wondered whether Gerard Wiekens remembered the Torpoint goal setting exercise in the summer of 98. They had done better than try, they went and nailed it!

Joe Royle really splashed the cash the following year to try and keep us up, shelling out around £15 million for the likes of Paolo Wanchope, Alfie

Haaland, Richard Dunne, Steve Howey and Darren Huckerby. Former World Footballer of the Year (and now well past his best) George Weah, even joined for a short stint on a free transfer.

Bish and Lee Crooks left for Miami and Barnsley with our gratitude.

Will went to a few games that season including taking his wife to her first Premier game, an awful 0-0 draw at Spurs. She didn't rush to come again!

The money spent failed to do the trick and City finished third bottom with a derisory 34 points. Relegation spelt the end of Joe Royle's reign with Kevin Keegan the high profile replacement.

Back in the second tier expectations were high that we would bounce back at the first attempt.

Signings including the free transfer capture of former England left-back legend Stuart 'Psycho' Pearce, Israeli Eyal Berkovic was paired with veteran Arabic Algerian play maker Ali Benarbia for City's very own central midfield United Nations.

Jon Macken arrived in February for an eyebrow raising £5 million, our new transfer record and what was to end up being as bad a piece of business as our previous record holder Lee Bradbury.

Shortly afterwards, Paul Dickov left for Leicester in the knowledge that he would always be an integral part of City's history. Legend!

City were the team to beat all season and won the League with 99 points, 10 more than second placed West Brom.

City renewed acquaintance with '99 foes Gillingham that season, winning both games comfortably. The Goat scored a hat-trick in one of those games and ended as City's top scorer for the third year running with 32 goals, in the process becoming the first City player to top 30 goals for City since Francis Lee in 1971.

On the last game of the season City played Portsmouth at Maine Road. The authors went to the game as records could have been broken with City needing to score four goals to break City's 108-goal League scoring record. It was also to be Stuart Pearce's last ever League game as the 39-year-old had announced his retirement from playing.

For the whole game, City fans shouted 'shoot' every time Pearce was on the ball anywhere near Pompey's goal. This was because he needed a goal to complete a century of career goals on his last chance to do so.

In the 90th minute, City who were leading 3-1, were awarded a really dubious penalty. The crowd bayed for Pearce to take it and a huge roar went up as he grabbed the ball and placed it on the spot. What a way to bow out, your 100th career goal and City breaking their scoring record at the same time.

Veteran goalkeeper Dave Beasant was in goal for Portsmouth and smiling he went up to Pearce and whispered something in his ear.

The crowd held its breath as Pearce took a typically aggressive run up, only to smash the ball way over the bar!

Later Beasant was asked what he had whispered in the ear of his former England colleague. He revealed, 'I told him that I would dive the wrong way and he just needed to get it on target!'

In five seasons we had experienced two relegations and three promotions. Some roller-coaster!

So City were once again in the Premier League for what would be their final season at Maine Road as they were due to move into the Commonwealth Games Stadium for the 2003-4 season.

Keegan really went to town with City's chequebook. The club transfer record was smashed to buy Nicholas Anelka from Paris St Germain for £13 million. Sylvain Distin had already arrived from PSG for £4 million as well as Vicente Vuoso from South America for £3.5 million (he was never to play a game for City!).

United's legendary goalkeeper Peter Schmeichel arrived on a free transfer and three more Wembley '99 heroes left; Jock Morrison, Terry Cooke and Richard Edghill all leaving on free transfers. Stuart Pearce joined Keegan's coaching staff.

In January City paid Leeds £6 million for Robbie Fowler, a move that threatened the place of the now worshipped Shaun Goater. City chairman David Bernstein resigned in protest at the excessive spending, claiming that we were putting City's financial future at risk. Director John Wardle took over as chairman.

There were several memorable games that season. The 2-1 home victory against Leeds where Mrs L. made her only ever visit to Manchester. Niclas Jensen scored a fantastic goal for City which Rania missed as she was searching for her gloves to warm her freezing hands! Girls – how can you possibly clap with gloves on!?

We won the final ever Maine Road derby match 3-1. Shaun Goater notched two to bring up his century of goals for the Blues. What a guy! Will remembers having a tear in his eye that day.

We drew 1-1 at Old Trafford, with an 86th minute equaliser and another derby goal from the Goat, less than a minute after he arrived from the subs bench. At the time it was a Premier League record for the quickest ever goal for a substitute.

Will went to the last two games to be played at Maine Road, both 1-0 defeats and both abject displays to bow out from the great stadium that had always been home for the authors and thousands of others. Martyn accompanied Will for the penultimate match, an awful defeat against West Ham and then Will was ecstatic to get a last minute ticket for the last ever match against Southampton, only to be disappointed again. Typical City!

This was to be the Goat's last ever match for City. The emotional farewell was the only saving grace of the otherwise let down day. Schmeichel played his last ever game that day too.

This meant that the last City scorer at Maine Road got his goal on Easter Monday, 21st April. It was scored by Marc Vivien Foé, who sadly collapsed and died just a few weeks later while playing for Cameroon. City rested his number 23 shirt forever as a mark of respect and to ensure, his name has appeared in every match day programme since.

City finished ninth that season, the first season for years that City fans could relax and enjoy the last few matches without worrying about promotion or relegation.

Even better, City qualified for the UEFA Cup via the Fair Play League, so European football would be coming to City's new stadium, the newly christened City Of Manchester Stadium, COMSTAD or Eastlands to the fans.

Big transfers included City fan Trevor Sinclair arriving for £2.5 million and former England stars David Seaman and Steve McManaman both arriving on free transfers. Sadly two more of the '99 boys left with Super Kevin Horlock joining West Ham and Jeff Whitley going to Sunderland.

Sinclair was to score the first competitive goal at COMSTAD, scored during a 5-0 UEFA Cup preliminary round victory against Welsh part-timers TNS. Will went as a guest of another TNS (Transaction Network Services) who had taken the Welsh club to their hearts.

Will also went to the 'real' first match, the Premier League game against Portsmouth. We again frustratingly let the scoring record go to an opponent with Yakubu recording the first League goal in the new stadium.

At least City salvaged a point with a 90th minute equaliser from French defender David Sommeil (ironically he was to nearly befall a similar fate to the last ever City Maine Road scorer Foé, collapsing on the pitch when training with his French club in 2008 and slipping into a coma. He since made something of a recovery but it is believed he still suffers poor health as a result of the incident).

The European adventure was to slip away without glory with an early round defeat on away goals against tiny Polish club Groclin Grodzisk. Will remembers watching the BBC text commentary while at Miami Airport of the goalless leg in Poland – really frustrating!

A memorable game that season was the 4-2 defeat at Portsmouth on 10th January, which was supposed to be Will's birthday treat. City sold Eyal Berkovic to Pompey the day before and incredibly allowed him to play in the game. Harry Redknap has obviously always been a good negotiator!

Of course Berkovic inspired Portsmouth to victory, even though City should never have lost and even hit the woodwork four times. The game was also memorable as it was David Seaman's last ever game, he picked up a bad injury early on and could not continue (ever again as it happened).

His replacement was Kevin Stuhr Ellegaard, a Danish short guy who rivalled Margetson as City's worst ever.

Happily a few days later we secured the services of England 'keeper David James for £2 million.

The following month, City played in one of the most amazing Cup games ever, an FA Cup fourth round replay at Spurs. Will watched in horror on TV as City went down 3-0 in the first half, lost star striker Anelka to injury and then had Joey Barton sent off for arguing as the players walked off for the half-time break.

Will was contemplating switching over to watch Jordan's antics in the jungle with Peter Andre but stuck with it for a while. He was rewarded in the 48th minute when City pulled one back. When City scored again after an hour, you could feel the nerves building up among the Spurs fans.

Ten man City equalised in the 80th minute through SWP and amazingly he crossed for Jon Macken to head the winner in the 90th minute. Probably the greatest ever FA Cup comeback!

City lost the next round at United but at least had the great pleasure of seeing Gary Neville sent off for a toddler-like temper tantrum!

We got revenge for that match by beating United 4-1 in the first ever Eastlands derby with SWP scoring a glorious breakaway fourth in the 90th minute. Despite these high profile successes, City were struggling in the League and flirting with relegation.

Bottom club Wolves came to Manchester on 10 April and led City 3-2 with time running out. A win for Wolves would have put City in real danger but as Will frantically kept refreshing his BBC text commentary while visiting friends in Athens, he was mightily relieved to see that SWP had equalised in the last minute.

Similarly, two weeks later City played at Leicester who were one of the few clubs below us and in the relegation zone. With the score 1-1, Leicester were awarded a very late penalty. As Will paced around his back garden, up stepped of all people Paul Dickov to take the penalty.

Surely not! He can't, can he? Thankfully David James saved the day. Will liked to think that Dicky just could not do it to us. Not before he had let out such a relieved yelp that his wife came running out to the garden fearing a pruning shears accident!

On 1 May and with games running out, City were still in grave danger, just three points and one place above the drop zone. That was the day of the

Newcastle home match and Will was in the crowd of over 47,000 packed into the stadium. The atmosphere was intense and the game closely contested.

When Paolo Wanchope scored what proved to be the winner in the second half, the crowd reacted as if we had won the League. It was a fabulous atmosphere for the entire game.

When Leeds lost the next day, City were definitely safe and eventually finished 17th, eight points clear of the drop zone. Why do City put us through it!?

We were broke again and before the 2004-05 season we signed four players for a total outlay of just £100,000!

Furthermore Nicholas Anelka was flogged to Fenerbahçe in Turkey for £7 million mid-season. Bernstein was being found to be correct when he said we were over-stretching ourselves with the Fowler purchase.

Gerard Wiekens was also released so only Nicky Weaver remained from the Gillingham Play-off victory, and he was barely playing due to a succession of injuries and loan spells elsewhere.

The season was pretty uneventful for much of the time even though it was an improvement on the previous seasons' struggles. We managed to beat would be champions Chelsea 1-0 thanks to Anelka.

The game was played in torrential rain and Will was receiving regular text updates while on a bus journey in Jordan. He got some pretty strange looks from the locals as he squirmed in his seat as Chelsea attacked incessantly looking for an equaliser.

With City pretty uninspiring all season, Keegan was sacked after a 1-0 defeat at home to Bolton in March left City in 12th.

Stuart Pearce took over as caretaker manager and City embarked on a run of great form that eventually meant that they needed to beat Middlesbrough at home on the last game of the season to pip them to a UEFA Cup spot for the following season.

The game was poised at 1-1 when City were awarded a penalty in the dying seconds. Score and City would qualify by rights for European football, miss and Boro would have the privilege.

Will watched in his lounge as *Gillette Soccer Saturday's* Paul Merson desribed the scene.

Robbie Fowler was putting the ball on the spot and Will paced round and round his lounge. Please, Please, Please! European football in any guise meant so much in those days.

'Up steps Fowler,' Merson teased, 'Oh no he's missed it Jeff!!!,' he screamed. 'Unbelievable.'

Will screamed back, 'YOU BA**ARD!' (aimed at Blobby Fowler not Merse).

Boro thus qualified for the UEFA Cup and were to go all the way to the Final in the following season. Will begrudged them every victory on their run!

City finished a creditable eighth despite the disappointment and Pearce was confirmed as full-time manager.

Just before the start of the 2005-06 season a bolt from the blue. Shaun Wright-Phillips wanted to join Chelsea. Our current favourite player and one real crumb of comfort during these times wanted to leave us. The player we had brought through the ranks after he was rejected by Forest and had turned into an England international, wanted out.

The authors were gutted, despite totally understanding why SWP should want to join Chelsea. He got his wish and we got £21 million in exchange. Good financial business all round for a player that cost us nothing. But the fans had lost our one creative spark and would gladly have returned the money to get our favourite son back.

That set the scene for the season, which was a real slog at times. City finished 15th, never really flirting with relegation but never looking like challenging for European places again either.

There were no really stand out games but there was one good example of Will's determination to see a City game no matter where he was and at the same time evidence of what his wife has to put up with.

They had a holiday to Morocco in the September of 2005 and it happened to coincide with the Old Trafford derby. After a nice couple of hours strolling around some picturesque and tranquil gardens, Will decided that he needed to find a bar showing the derby.

He then frog marched his wife along a busy highway in 45° heat on what appeared to be a long, thirsty and fruitless mission. They bundled into a convenience store to buy some much-needed water to be confronted by four United shirted Moroccans watching the match.

They had walked in right on half-time, just as United took the lead and the locals went mad!

We were invited to stay and watch the second half with them, which Will enthusiastically accepted while Rania just sighed. Water soon turned to beer of course.

Will was quite restrained when Joey Barton equalised in the second half, managing to keep his fist pumping confined to his pocket.

So a 1-1 draw and honours even, despite the fact that United had dominated the game. Will left wishing his North African friends good luck for the rest of the season (not meaning a word of it) to take Rania for a nice meal to make up for her endurance!

In May 2006 one favourite son did return. Paul Dickov came on a free-transfer from Blackburn to be in our squad for the 2006-07 season.

Dicky, who was now a full Scotland international, was never a prolific goalscorer and he was joining a club devoid of attacking flair and with no money once more.

Dickov was beset by injuries in his second spell and only managed 16 appearances (seven as substitute) and didn't score a goal. They say you should never go back, and this was a definite example where this was a correct assertion.

We finished the season in 14th and only scored 29 goals all season making us joint lowest scorers with bottom club Watford. Dire.

Stuart Pearce was sacked enabling him to become full-time England Under-21 manager (a post he had unsuccessfully tried to combine with managing City).

Paul Dickov left the club once more and with Nicky Weaver's free transfer departure to Charlton, the team of '99 were all just a City fan's memory. But what fantastic memories they were…

So what of the heroes of 2012? Cynics call them mercenaries, only at City for the cash. While true that money talks, they are winners too. City winners at that.

The authors expect City to go from strength to strength. Sheikh Mansoor seems totally committed to continue his 'project' and like Roman Abramovic at Chelsea, he will surely crave the Champions League.

The Sheikh makes Roman look like a pauper in comparison and he has a mission beyond football. That is to turn his homeland of Abu Dhabi into a household name throughout the world. They have their Grand Prix, they have their International Cricket Ground, they have their Tourist Board and they have their Football Club. That club is City.

Despite the UEFA Financial Fair Play Regulations, there is no reason why City can't build upon the successes of the past two seasons and win trophy after trophy, including the big one, the Champions League.

But what if the Arab money dried up? What if the Sheikh and City parted company?

Would it be Armageddon with City facing bankruptcy like Glasgow Rangers and forced to re-build from the bottom or would there be a legacy of funds, facilities and hope left behind?

City fans will have their own thoughts on this but here is the $64 million question. We kept the faith before when we were flat broke, we followed the boys home and away in the third tier of football, but would we do it again?

Would it be a case of, 'if I hadn't seen such riches I could live with being poor' (acknowledgement to the lyrics of James; the band not David!) or would it be City 'Til I Die and Keep The Faith?'

The authors sincerely hope we never have to answer that question.

City 'Til We Die!

The 2012/13 Season

It took weeks to come down from the euphoria.

That was the most amazing finish to any season. Only the 1989 climax to the old first division came even remotely close. That was when Arsenal needed to win 2 nil at Anfield to pip Liverpool and did thanks to Michael Thomas's late late strike.

Our victory was even more amazing. Never before had the top league in England been decided by goal difference and due to a goal in the third minute of stoppage time at that. Oh, and to pip your near neighbours and reviled rivals just to add more spice to the mix.

The media were lapping it up. United had choked it but City deserved their win due to their free flowing brand of football that had brought so many goals said most observers.

Others called City lucky and pointed out that they had only just managed to master a decidedly average United.

Whatever. We were just determined to enjoy the moment and rub their noses in it at every opportunity.

The challenge now was to retain the League and do well in Europe.

Roberto Mancini signed a new five-year contract as reward for the trophies and to ward off rumoured overtures from Paris St Germain.

We were confident of retaining the Title. After all, they signed Phil Jones, we signed Kun Agüero!

As it happened it was to be more telling that they signed Robin van Persie (RVP) and we signed Scott Sinclair. Mancini was clearly livid that we had failed to deliver any of his prime transfer targets – RVP had left Arsenal for our dear neighbours (despite Mancini being convinced he had agreed to come to City), Eden Hazard who joined Chelsea from Lille, Javi Martinez who left Spain for Bayern and Edinson Cavani who remained in Naples.

He openly fell out with Sporting Director Brian Marwood over what he considered his abject failure to deliver any top target when we just needed a quality addition or two to kick on again and leave the rest trailing in our wake. Tensions had started to surface before a ball had been kicked in anger.

Most people agreed that we were weaker squad wise this term and last - out went winners Adam Johnson and Nigel de Jong to be replaced by inferior players. As well as Sinclair, other pre-season signings were midfielder Jack Rodwell from Everton, right back Maicon from Inter, Nastasić, the 19 year-old Serbian centre-back from Fiorentina, Spain international midfielder Javi Garcia from Benfica and Richard Wright as squad (i.e. never to play) goalkeeper.

Stefan Savic left as part of the Nastasić deal but all in all, we had still spent a cool £50m.

The season started with the Community Shield, played at Villa Park due to Teams GB playing their London 2012 games at Wembley (Naturally both GB teams bowed out in the QFs, the Stuart Pearce managed chaps inevitably on penalties).

The Olympics were to have added significance for City as their only representative in the men's team Micah Richards was injured in a group match, effectively ruling him out of almost the entire season. This paved the way for the fan's favourite Pablo Zabaleta, to take City's right-back berth for his own and to grow into the Prem's best player in that position.

Back to the Community Shield, this was to be a game that was to aptly define our season - scintillating at times but wasteful in front of goal. City were left hanging on at the end despite dominating for 90% of the match.

A 3-2 win against FA Cup holders and European champions Chelsea, brought home the Shield in this glorified friendly. We had lost the previous season's curtain raiser by the same scoreline but went on to win the Prem - was this a bad omen? Reverse karma?

They say that 111 is an unlucky number. It is known as 'Nelson' in cricket, depicting the fact that the great admiral had taken a few for his country so that by the end of his days he only had one eye, one arm and one ball (in the genitalia sense!) In cricket circles it is a time when wickets are said to fall and many will remember that umpire David Shepherd used to superstitiously stand on one leg whenever any team reached 111, 222, 333 etc.

This was City's 111th season as a league club – another bad omen?

Enough of such hogwash and on to the first game of the season, at home against newly promoted Southampton. In what was to become a nasty habit, we played as if we had a divine right to win.

The 3-2 victory came at great cost with Kun injured early doors and facing a lengthy lay off. The joint favourite for the Golden Boot was to have a stop start season, further exacerbating Mancini's ire at missing out on RVP.

Will watched the game after sneaking into the lounge during a friend's barbecue on a roasting hot day in August. By the end of the match there were more people that had joined him than remained in the garden eating burgers, attracted by the fact that City were 2-1 down.

The impression was that City had used up all their goodwill from fans of other clubs and now we were being lumped together with United, Chelsea and Arsenal as just another title winning club and there to be shot down. Such progress!

The win against the Saints was our third consecutive win by the odd goal in five - not for the faint hearted. City fans saw the close game as a mere sign of ring rustiness. The normal service of home domination and huge away wins would be resumed shortly.

It never really panned out this way with the free scoring exploits of the previous season soon just a memory.

Unconvincing in the league and dumped out of the League Cup at the first hurdle despite being drawn at home to struggling Villa, we were all pinning our hopes on a better Champions League campaign.

We had been drawn in the group of death. Our co-efficient (European ranking) was such that we were 2nd seeds despite being champions of one of the toughest leagues in Europe and this saw us drawn with Real Madrid (Spanish champs), Ajax (Dutch number one) and Borussia Dortmund (German Bundesliga title holders).

We started the campaign in the Bernebau, home of Madrid. With a few minutes remaining we led 2-1 with goals from Džeko and an 85th minute free kick from Kolarov. Such fun! This year would be different - it was, however much worse!

Madrid soon equalized and Ronaldo of all people got a late winner and that knocked the stuffing right out of us. Hart criticised the players openly for their lack of professionalism in throwing away the lead instead of keeping possession for the last 5 minutes. Mancini criticised Hart for his honesty.

City finished bottom of the group with three fortunate home draws being all we had to show for our efforts - the first time an English club had failed to win a single CL group game.

Will saw every one of the six group games - 3 on TV (including the Dortmund home game in a small smoky bar in Bulgaria with a pumping techno soundtrack replacing any commentary) and 3 live. This included his first ever CL away trip in Amsterdam.

Before the game there was trouble in the red-light district, with 22 police riot vans to take away 20 arrested fans. Plenty of room to stretch shackled legs!

A good number of Blues enjoyed a few good-natured beers in Dam Square before the hike up to the Centraal Station for the train to Amsterdam ArenA.

It was very amusing watching the worse for wear City fans trying to work out the Dutch ticket and travel instructions but everybody get there OK.

Will was sat with the Ajax fans having failed to get a City end ticket and heard from his mates Burfield and Coope that City fans had been treated like cattle, herded through 2 small turnstiles.

City took the lead through Nasri, Ajax equalised just before half time and then capitalised on uncertainty in City's 3 centre-half defence to score 2 without even the hint of a reply in the 2nd half.

Post match, players complained of not understanding their defensive roles in the fluid zonal-marking system.

Cracks were appearing and Mancini had failed target number one of getting us through the group. We would have to up the pace of our Prem title defence if we were to reach target number two.

In what was to prove a significant moment, Txiki Begiristain became Director of Football in October with Marwood 'demoted' to Academy Director. City had already brought in Ferran Soriano as CEO with the pair old colleagues at Barcelona where they had played a significant part in the Catalan club's success.

The new regime would want their own man in charge and rumours immediately circulated that Mancini was not that man and that Pep Guardiola, on a sabbatical away from football, would re-join his old bosses in swapping Barca for City.

We were still misfiring in the Prem – Mrs. L (wearing her Mancini replica shirt!) and husband saw City draw 1-1 at home to Arsenal with the returning Agüero missing an absolute sitter. The entertainment value had been dire.

Our wins were hard-fought at this time with Džeko earning supersub status after a late winner at Fulham and a late brace at West Brom to earn 10-man City an unlikely win.

Aptly Will had been in Sarajevo, Edin's birthplace, for the late Craven Cottage coup de grace.

Wearing his City shirt, Will came to realise what a hero he is in his homeland as locals came up and congratulated him and asked if he lived near the great man!

His Bosnian international shirt was the number one available to buy in the Old Town market, outstripping Messi and Ronaldo 3 to 1 and he was shown as the poster boy advertising the up-coming World Cup qualifier against Greece.

Džeko and his TV actress and model partner Amra Silajdzic are the Posh and Becks of Bosnia and had even been the guests of honour alongside Angelina Jolie at the Sarajevo Film Festival.

After the West Brom win, Will attended City's next 2 away league matches – an entertaining nil-nil at West Ham and a boring goalless draw at Chelsea. The second match was notable as being Rafa Benitez's first match in charge as interim Chelsea manager following the departure of European Champion Roberto Di Matteo.

Never before has a home manager been booed so roundly as the bewildered Spaniard. It was only the announcement of the death of former Stamford Bridge manager Dave Sexton that silenced the resounding jeers. Devine intervention for Rafa!

We were still unbeaten but had drawn 5 out of 13 compared with the previous unbeaten start to the season when we had won 12 out of 14.

A couple of weeks later came the big one at the Etihad. City had not lost at home for 37 games (the 2nd longest run in Premier League history). Blues confidently expected this to stretch to 38 as United came to town.

In the event we were two down by half time but pulled back to 2-2 with a late Zabaleta equaliser and were in the ascendency with the whiff of an unlikely victory in our nostrils.

When the Rags got a last minute free kick within shooting range we held our breath. Up stepped RVP who fired towards the defensive wall.

Nasri ducked to avoid spoiling his coiffed bonce and the ball flew past the unsighted Hart into the corner of the onion bag.

The Linsdell lounge was livid. All sorts of expletives were aimed at the cowardly Frenchman. Why the heck had he ducked? If he had taken one in the moosh for the lads he would have been a hero. As it was he was pilloried as a wimp of the highest order.

United had won to take a 6 point lead at the top, smash City's unbeaten home record and put down a huge Premier League statement of intent. The wounded animal was biting back and was to never look back from this pivotal victory.

Team	P	W	D	L	GF	GA	GD	PTS
Manchester United	16	13	0	3	40	23	17	39
Manchester City	16	9	6	1	30	14	16	33
Chelsea	16	8	5	3	28	17	11	29
Everton	16	6	8	2	27	20	7	26
Tottenham H	16	8	2	6	29	25	4	26

The Mancini rhetoric was that City hadn't deserved to lose, that we would bounce back. Deep down City fans wondered if this was already misguided defiance. We were just not the same article as the previous season despite this being our first defeat.

A week later we had the most eagerly awaited BBC Sports Personality of the Year ever.

In the year of London 2012, gold medal winners Bradley Wiggins, Mo Farrah, Ellie Simmons, Kath Grainger and Jessica Ennis vied with Grand Slam winner and Gold medallist Andy Murray and Major winner Rory McIlroy for the individual award whilst Team GB and the Ryder Cup winners vied for team of the year.

The football section was longer than usual with Vinnie and Kun on hand with the Prem Trophy as the dramatic finale of the previous season was re-lived. As the star duo entered the fray carrying the trophy, Blue Moon rang out and the whole audience (hopefully including David Beckham) turned their backs and did the Poznan. Absolute class!

This really wound up fans of United - and they call us bitter!

That was probably the highlight of December for us with Christmas festivities spoiled once again by a completely unwarranted one-nil defeat at Sunderland yet again, on Boxing Day – the winning goal scored by Adam Johnson naturally!

January went pretty well but United more than matched us results wise to retain their lead.

Significantly we won at Arsenal for the first time since 1975. Remarkably Milner & Džeko became our first match-winners there since Asa Hartford, Joe Royle & Rodney Marsh earned us a 3-2 victory 38 years before!

The Gunners had a man sent off early doors and we strolled to a 2 nil win, made more difficult by Kompany's unjust dismissal mid way through the 2nd half.

In a déjà vu moment we were to be shorn of our skipper as well as Yaya (on African Nations Cup duty once more) for most of January.

This time however, Vinnie's red card was universally decried as a wrong decision. Perhaps most significantly Lineker, Hansen and Savage all vociferously said as much. The red was rescinded - oh the power of the media!

In an ironic twist, Kompany got injured two weeks later and went on to miss many more games than he would have been suspended for!

Mario Balotelli took real centre stage for City in January, despite not featuring for the first team.

He had already threatened to take City to a football tribunal in December as the club had fined him 2 weeks wages for his poor 2011-12 disciplinary record that had seen him miss 11 games through suspension. He decided to drop his claim apparently out of respect to the City fans and Roberto Mancini.

In early January he had a public bust-up with Mancini on City's Carrington training pitch. The papers were full of pictures and headlines claiming it to be the end for Super Mario at City. Apparently Mancini had objected to a tough tackle on Scott Sinclair by the enigmatic Italian and had squared up to the striker.

It was to be the beginning of the end. Mancini, so often Mario's defence for his hair-brain actions, had run out of excuses and bowed to pressure to allow him to leave. The father/son style relationship that they enjoyed was severed once more.

Balotelli left for AC Milan at the end of January after a typically drawn out transfer saga for around £20m. He was mobbed by the Rossoneri fans everywhere he went and promptly rewarded them with a winning a double on his Milan debut, including a trademark coolly taken penalty.

So after 79 appearances in all competitions for City, 29 goals, 21 yellow cards, 4 red cards, several tantrums, dozens of stories of bizarre behaviour, consistently erratic play and the endearing ability to wind-up United, the oddball that is Mario Balotelli finally left these shores after two and a half seasons. Will he return one day? The journalists certainly hope so!

Back to mundane matters, the league was to be a pipedream from mid February on. Our January surge was scuppered by a frustrating midweek 0-0 at QPR at the end of the month. We dominated for 90 minutes in atrocious conditions but found Cesar in inspired form in goal.

Will had now been to 3 London away games at a cost of £170 and not seen a single goal! Getting soaked on the walk to Shepherd's Bush station was the final insult.

Worse was to follow. In early February we travelled to Southampton for a teatime kick off – Will attended St Mary's with his fellow Exeter City devotee mate Chris.

What City served up would have been hard-pressed to defeat the League Two City.

Calamitous defensive howlers from Hart and Gareth Barry and the comedy own goal of the year from the hapless Barry saw us fall to a 3-1 defeat.

The performance was abject. It was if we were doing an impression of Martyn Margetson, Rae Ingram, Alan Kernighan, Jim Whitley, Adie Mike and Craig Russell et al for old time's sake.

Chris turned to Will as they supped post-match beers and remarked that as a neutral he had just witnessed a team without spirit and clearly not in harmony with each other. Oh dear!

That was just about that as far as the Prem was concerned. 12 points behind with 12 games left. Our goose was cooked and the race was run.

Team	P	W	D	L	GF	GA	GD	PTS
Manchester United	26	21	2	3	62	31	31	65
Manchester City	26	15	8	3	48	24	24	53
Chelsea	26	14	7	5	55	28	27	49
Tottenham H	26	14	6	6	44	30	14	48
Arsenal	26	12	8	6	50	29	21	44

We tried to convince ourselves otherwise of course. We had overturned 8 points with 5 to play last season after all. The difference this season was that United did not ever look like slipping up. RVP was banging them in for fun and De Gea was starting to look like a Premier League goalie at last.

City were in fact to remain 2nd for the rest of the season with the gap to United staying in double figures from then on.

The only thing worth smiling about for City in the spring this time around was the player's rendition of the Harlem Shake, the dance craze that had swept the Internet. Rather than describing the bonkers phenom-enon, readers should log on to the MCFC website to look for themselves at City's Joe Hart choreographed version. Legendary kitman Les Chapman is hilarious!

Back to the pitch, despite the war being won by United, City did win one significant battle courtesy of a dominant 2-1 victory at Old Trafford on a Monday night in early April. Goals from James Milner and a wonderful strike from Kun gave us a deserved win when man for man, City proved they were better than United on their day. If only their day had come more often!

Final Table	P	W	D	L	GF	GA	GD	PTS
Manchester United	38	28	5	5	86	43	43	89
Manchester City	38	23	9	6	66	34	32	78
Chelsea	38	22	9	7	75	39	36	75
Arsenal	38	21	10	7	72	37	35	73
Tottenham H	38	21	9	8	66	46	20	72

Sweet FA Cup?

With the Premier League defence pretty much over by February, our season's salvation and presumably that of Roberto Mancini lay in the FA Cup, the trophy that began our rise.

City marched all the way to the semi-final without conceding a goal with wins against Watford, Stoke, Leeds and Barnsley.

This gave us a Wembley semi-final against Chelsea, who had overcome United in the quarter-final after a replay.

Will's local Supporters Club came up with the goods and Mrs L. & he left at midday for the big trip – plenty of time to meet Geoff Coope in Marylebone for a pre-match beer or three.

Will had been to AFC Wimbledon the previous day to see Exeter City and the hosts fight out an entertaining 2-2 draw. There cannot have been too many people that went to the Cherry Records Stadium on the Saturday and Wembley on the Sunday.

Arriving at their suburban station they found chaos. Some poor soul had decided to end it all in South Croydon – there would be no trains into London at all for the next few hours.

Luckily there was plenty of time and Will had local knowledge. They therefore skipped the huge bus queues outside the station and headed to a different stop to wait for a bus to Croydon as Will knew there would be trains on a different line to London from West Croydon.

The journey was tortuous as along the route hundreds of other stranded train passengers tried to make progress.

When Will and Rania got to West Croydon there was a sea of people and the platforms were closed due to over-crowding. It was here that they met Graham Hooper and his son, City fans both who were also Wembley bound. Graham was proudly wearing one of Willie Donachie's old shirts!

Cue two cheeky chappie Chelsea fans, both hyper for some reason! They knew a bloke that had a seven seater who would get all six to Wimbledon for train from there. Unfortunately the people carrier owner was out apparently. No problem, one of them was best mates with the owner of a local taxi firm. No taxis available for at least 2 hours!

It seemed that other people were a step ahead today. With plan A, B & C bust, plan D was a tram to Wimbledon. The small group yomped to the nearest tram stop 15 minutes away. It was now 1.15 PM and time to grab a couple of cans of beer – Marylebone was seeming a step too far now for a pre-match drink and everyone just wanted to get to Wembley.

Safely on the tram and inspiration. Will suddenly realised you could get off at Mitcham Junction, get a train to Elephant & Castle and then a tube to Wembley.

The two Chelsea geezers were still being hyper. Cracking jokes, telling each other off for swearing in front of women and children, telling the same stories three times and saying hi to strangers. The fact that they believed kick-off was 5.15 and not 4pm spoke volumes. They only believed it when checking their tickets.

The group became City only at Elephant as the Chelsea pair dived into a local pub – it would not have surprised anybody if that was where they stayed.

The train from Baker Street was full of Chelsea fans throwing celary. Mrs L. was bemused by this and not impressed at the celary/Wembley link!

Wembley loomed into sight around 3, author and wife wished Graham and lad good luck, consumed some expensive stadium beer and fish & chips and took their seats to enjoy the pre-match atmosphere.

It was sunglasses weather and City served up some sunshine football, totally dominating for an hour and going two up through Nasri and Kun and seemingly cruising to victory as chances were spurned to kill the game completely.

Rafa, still universally unpopular at the Bridge, sent on Torres for Mikel after 66 minutes and almost immediately Ba reduced the arrears with a typical wonder strike.

Despite a couple of lung-busting breakaways and near misses from Yaya, we were now hanging on. Chelsea should have had a penalty and it was a mighty relief when Chris Foy blew for full time.

City would play Wigan in the final with City swiftly installed as the hottest favourites for years.

The Wembley build-up did not however go quite as planned. City secured Champions League qualification by squeaking past West Brom 1-0 but suddenly one thing dominated the headlines, front and back page.

Sir Alex announced his shock retirement from Nitid and football management at the end of the season after what would be an amazing and insurmountable 1,500 games in charge.

Whatever you say about Ferguson (and the author has said plenty of deregoatory things about him over the years), you cannot deny that he has the greatest managerial record of all time. Enough said.

The author had actually predicted the end and tweeted as such on 12th April (see below).

Will Linsdell @wilburthewotsit	12 Apr

I reckon SAF will announce shock retirement at end of season - losing his marbles!

Expand ← Reply ⨝ Retweet ★ Favorite ••• More

He seemed to be feigning enjoyment at winning and ironically claiming the title so easily probably quelled the fire in his belly. Comments like RVP could have been killed by a football hitting his head showed some flawed thinking and he appeared to have had a couple of glasses before every interview.

He had taken the CL quarter-final defeat against Madrid to heart and with the rise of the German clubs probably realised that another CL was beyond him.

Many City fans said good riddance, but deep down the majority will miss the love-to-hate figure.

The last thunder stealing headline in the build up to Wembley was the strong rumour emanating from Spain that Mancini would be sacked, win or lose the final, with Malaga's Chilean coach Manuel Pellegrini taking over. The bookmaker odds for this to happen plummeted to 20-1 on. It broke on the Friday evening and refused to die down.

So was the guy that had delivered our first trophy in 35 years and our first ever Prem title on his way out?

Twitter went into overdrive. Forza Mancini being the overwhelming sentiment.

Surely this was a wind up? Silence from the City hierarchy. No denial or vote of confidence from Ferrano or Bergistran. Oh my god, its true!

Our hot favouritism was perhaps misguided, as our form leading up to the final was not great. We had scraped an undeserved 1-0 win against Wigan in the Prem thanks to a fabulous Tevez strike, drawn nil-nil at nothing to play for Swansea and in the game prior to the final had scored that undeserved victory at home to West Brom.

We were not firing at all despite all our big guns and the Mancini rumours would only hinder matters for City.

Will had managed to get a ticket for the final courtesy of his old City mate Harvey 'Mainstand' Clarke so would be sat with Geoff and Mad Lawrence, a real late 80s\early 90's throwback supporting and banter wise. Harvey had stupidly booked a holiday in Corfu that clashed.

Will and his Devonian pals had travelled together many times before, meeting up at Exeter Services from their Devon homes for the 10 hour round trip for 90 minutes at Maine Road. These were the days of Uwe, Quinny, Kinky, Ooh Curley Whirley, Paul Walsh, Terry Phelan and Tony Coton as well as our

Wonderkids Lakey, Whitey, Hinchy, Golden Moulden, Stevie Redmond and Ian Brightwell.

They were barren years but superb fun. The days of the City Chippy, the Beehive & Sherwood pubs, the Social Club with Big Helen (of the bell fame) demanding you buy a draw ticket in her gravelly Manchester growl and the souvenir shop no bigger than a couple of sheds. Happy days!

Now it was a different City but the same sense of humour. Still self-deprecating and still supporting a club prone to the odd cock-up. Cue the Mancini rumours just before the Cup Final.

Will met Lawrence and Geoff at a Marylebone pub for pre-match beers. All the talk was of mini-bus trips of the past and Mancini's future. All present unanimously wanted him to stay.

In a crass devaluation of the 'world's greatest cup competition', there were league games that day with Chelsea, still with a chance of leapfrogging us for 2nd place, playing relegation threatened Villa in the lunch-time kick off.

Will and mates decided to take in the last 20 minutes at the Marylebone Sports Bar by the station.

As they witnessed Frank Lampard score a late winner to break the Chelsea all time scoring record, they noticed a special guy watching with his wife and kids.

None other than Shaun 'The Goat' Goater! A true City legend with over 100 goals for the club, the 99th robbing Gary Neville on the touchline before stroking the ball home from a tight angle and the 100th dinking over Batty Barthez in the same game to register a 3-1 win in the final Maine Road derby.

There he stood - too good an opportunity to miss. He remembered the 98 friendly at Torpoint and the sports quiz won by Will, Martyn and Gerard Wiekens. Legend. He happily posed for photos.

So on to Wembley. What should have been an enjoyable day out for Bobby Manc leading his team out at Wembley had turned into a nightmare.

Pre-match interviews were not focusing on his formation or pre-match meal but on his future. He was forced to say they were rubbish when deep down he knew his days were numbered. He stated that he didn't know why City had been speaking with Pellegrini's agent - he did of course.

The City faithful were defiant in their support for the Italian – "Mancini, He comes from Italy. To manage Man City. Mancini, Mancini." We loved him and wanted him to stay.

Will had broken the rumours to Mrs. L the morning of the match and she was very upset at the unjust prospect.

Mancini pulled a surprise before kick off. Having played Pantilimon in goal for every round up until the final, he chose Hart. This was as much about Mancini the disciplinarian as Mancini the tactician.

Big Pants had given an interview that week to Romanian media in which he admitted that his future probably lay away from City. As soon as he made that comment he surely sealed his Final fate.

So it was to be Wigan that stood between City and silverware. Nice guys with Dave Whelan their honorable chairman and Roberto Martinez their likeable manager.

City outnumbered their fans 3 to 1. Will had detected an air of complacency amongst the fans. Would it be 3 or 4 nil?

This complacency was reciprocated on the pitch. City players performed like they thought they just had to show up whilst Wigan knew this was their one and only chance for glory and played that way.

As the game wore on and Wigan became more and more comfortable letting City have possession without doing a lot with it, the volume from their fans grew noticeably as they really started to believe they could do it.

When Zaba was sent off for 2 bookable offences late on, they really believed it. And they were right to.

With stoppage time ebbing away at the end, Clichy desperately conceded a corner to stop the marauding McManaman, who had terrorised him all day, from getting a cross in.

The corner came over, substitute Ben Watson beat Jack Rodwell to the ball and guided an unstoppable header past Hart. Game over.

City fans applauded the Wigan fans and players. They had deserved it. The neutral in us was pleased for Dave Whelan, an absolute stalwart who truly loves not just Wigan the football club but Wigan the town too.

Will tweeted as much #longlivetheunderdog and received plaudits for being magnanimous. He was hurting like hell really and very angry towards the players. It was like they had betrayed Mancini and done it on purpose to bang in the final nail in the coffin of his City career.

Will got soaked walking to the train. The final ignominy of an awful day.

Post-match Mancini offered no excuses for the poor performance but criticised the City hierarchy for their lack of support of him. The words of a man resigned to his fate.

The media speculation went into overdrive before an official club statement posted late Monday evening confirmed that Mancini and City had parted company.

Apparently he didn't fit our requirements for a holistic approach and focus on youth development.

The media said it was due to falling out with star players like Hart, Kompany, Silva and Richards. There was certainly no love lost with the City execs.

The red tops lapped it up with their character assassination, interviewing some former City kitboy numpty who twisted the knife, painting every word as gospel.

Will was cross with the club at the way they handled it all. Lack of respect for a manager that will always be special to the fans. Too much like Chelsea for Will's liking.

At least it deflected the media away from their Fergie love fest as the red nosed one approached retirement, even if only for a day or two.

In a final act of defiance, Mancini paid for a full page in the Manchester Evening News thanking the fans for three unforgettable years and stating we would always have a place in his heart.

It was a class act and at the same time a two-fingered salute to the City hierarchy. He will always be up there with Joe and Big Mal in the eyes of the fans. Moneyed yes but still the man who created history.

City fans (including the author) reciprocated by clubbing together to raise £7,000 to place an advert thanking Mancini in the Italian publication,

La Gazetta dello Sport. Adam Keyworth started the 'Grazie Mancini' ball rolling via his Twitter feed and soon had enough to pay for the insertion and also make a sizeable donation to a Manchester charity.

Another example of the class of us City fans!

Blues supporters have a lot to thank Mancini for - the 6-1 at Trafford, 5-1 at Spurs, the Cup and Prem, winding up Fergie and Moyes etc.

Most of all for Will, he got his wife following City in earnest and he just hopes that her interest continues, although it is doubtful she will want Pellegrini on the back of her next shirt!

City had a league game on the following Tuesday at Reading. Will's first reaction after the Wigan defeat was to rip up the ticket he had for the match, but this now took on added significance with Mancini's departure and there was still a point needed to secure 2nd place.

Will met up with Geoff for the game, played throughout in the pouring rain. Italian flags and banners abounded - Grazie Mancini and Forza Mancini. The Italian's name rang out throughout.

Brian Kidd was in charge for the game and cut a lone figure in the dugout due to the fact that David Platt and City's small army of Italian coaches had followed Bobby Manc out of the door.

City won 2 nil to secure that 2nd spot with goals from Kun and Edin. On the same night Wigan lost at Arsenal to condemn them to relegation. What a few days for the Cup finalists!

City lost their final game of the season, 3-2 at home to Norwich. The significant scoreline had happened again, only this time against City. Perhaps this was a fitting end to the season. At least Mancini got a rousing reception in his absence.

The game was significant as Mark Halsey's last ever match as a referee. City fans applauded him warmly – if it had not been for those 5 added minutes back in 1999, we would not be where we are today. Thank you Mark – if it had only been 4 minutes, where may we be now?

Not too much to shout about there then from the 2012/13 season despite 2nd place and Champions League qualification, together with the Shield and FA Cup runners-up medals.

Oh how we would have dreamed of a season like that only a few years ago and now here we were, disappointed. It is to be sincerely hoped that City fans never get complacent or worst still arrogant like United and Chelsea. Please no.

Individuals wise, Joe Hart picked up the Golden Glove for most clean-sheets for the third successive season and Pablo Zabaleta was named Premier League best right-back at the PFA awards (and is/was a dead-cert for City's player of the year award).

Compare this to the previous season when Hart, Kompany, Silva and Yaya had all featured in that team of the year and Vinnie was Sports Writer's Player of the Year.

This season we were just left scratching our heads as to why Nastasić hadn't made the Young Player of the Year shortlist (he had kept Lescott out for most of the season with his mature displays despite only being 19) and were completely perplexed how Rio Ferdinand had made the Premier League Team of the Year, when he would not have come close to making the City 1st Team.

At least Gareth Bale pipped RVP for the Player of the Year trophy.

Matija Nastasić was now a regular for City and Serbia (playing alongside United's Vidic) and is widely regarded as easily City's best signing the previous summer. Wearing the same number 33 that captain fantastic Vincent Kompany wore on his debut season, he has looked commanding and confident way beyond his years and set for a prolonged stay in the City team. Bad news for Joleon & Kolo.

Apart from that, of the new signings Rodwell looked like he could be a good signing as evidenced by his two well-taken goals at home to Norwich that earned him an England call-up. If only he can stay fit.

The jury's still out on Garcia – not as dominant as De Jong was for City and not good enough to displace Barry. Maybe the season will do him good and he will be much improved come August 2013.

Maicon & Sinclair have been under-utilised and under-whelming, whilst Wright has performed the goalkeeping. understudy's understudy as well as his predecessor in the role, Stuart Taylor (answers on a postcard as to what exactly he is paid to do!)

So what of 2013/14? It looks nailed on that Pellegrini will have arrived by the time this is being read and City are being linked with the likes of Cavani, Isco and Fernandinho, all very hot properties. The Chilean should be looking forward to it as much as a kid with free-reign in Thorntons!

The financial fair play regulations still loom large of course but the City brand seems to be growing stronger and stronger with the announcement of a tie up with minority shareholders New York Yankees to jointly own a US MSL franchise team to be known as New York City. They will start playing in 2015 in a clear move to expand City's global appeal and therefore turnover.

There are plans to extend the Etihad to accommodate over 60,000 fans and a major shirt sponsorship deal has been struck with Nike, reportedly worth £72million over six years.

Add in the hugely impressive training and academy complex being built, and you can see that the owners mean business and will be creating a lasting legacy.

All a far cry from 1998!

MANCHESTER CITY F.C.

THE CITIZENS

1976-77 LEAGUE DIVISION ONE
AND CUP

Will's 1st City Season Scrapbook – City Finished 2nd &
Then Along Came Big Mal...

Above: The author with the Premier League Trophy and the Community Shield

Left: The author meets Sky's Robbie Savage in Amsterdam prior to the Ajax game (Gary Neville was suitably ignored!)

Above: Mrs L at the Etihad before the Arsenal game (her choice of red jacket!)

Left: And at Wembley for the semi-final against Chelsea

The author with The Goat!

The Harlem Shake, City style

Left: Mario & Mancini's Bust-up

Below: Weekend of Contrast

THE FA CUP WITH BUDWEISER

2013 **SEMI-FINAL**

MAN UNITED/CHELSEA
V MANCHESTER CITY

14 APRIL 2013
ENTRANCES OPEN 2:00PM
KICK OFF 4:00PM
ENTRANCE   M
BLOCK   130
ROW   13
SEAT   230
MANCHESTER CITY
           50.00   FULL PRICE

9075602   WEMBLEY

9075602
1098466

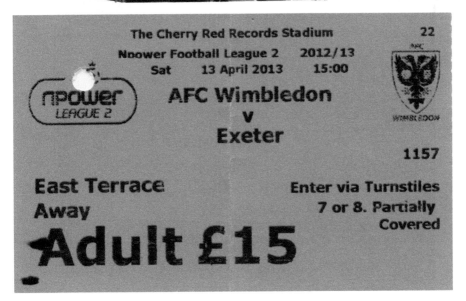

The Cherry Red Records Stadium   22

Npower Football League 2   2012/13
Sat   13 April 2013   15:00

AFC Wimbledon
v
Exeter

1157

East Terrace
Away

Enter via Turnstiles
7 or 8. Partially
Covered

Adult £15

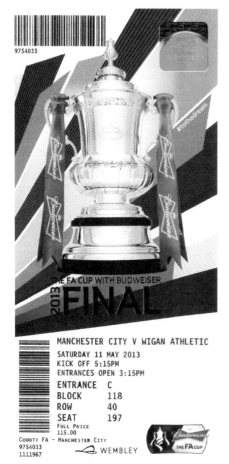

Left: My First FA Cup Final Attended (Better Luck Next Time!)

Below: Manchester Evening News

City fans show their feelings at Reading – we sang his name throughout

Ilicic ha detto sì alla Fiorentina

E i viola scelgono l'uruguaiano Munua come secondo portiere. Il Catania vuole Kurtic

Al Verona fumata grigia con Mandorlini Oggi incontro Corini-Chievo

GRAZIE
MANCINI

Per sempre uno di noi
Once a blue, always a blue

★ ★ ★

Manchester City
Supporters

And in print in the Italian press